THE EARTH SCHOOL GUIDE TO MIND SPIRIT MAPPING

The Earth School Guide to Mind Spirit Mapping

A COMPLETE GUIDE TO REMEMBERING YOUR PURPOSE

Sarah Breen

Leslie Baker - Illustrator

Earth School Shaman

Thank you to all who picked up this book. Without curiosity and a willingness to deepen our understanding of ourselves, we cannot better the future that bears our choices by default.

To the ancestors, thank you for getting us here. For without you, your discipline, blood, sweat, and tears, we would not have the choices we do today. However, we perceive it is in how we live it.

To my boys, Liam and Owen, and husband Kevin, without our dance together, I would not strive every day to be better than the last.

- Sarah Breen, Earth School Shaman

Contents

Dedication		v
Preface		ix

About the Cover — **1**

	Introduction	3
1	What Happened?	5
2	Asking the Right Questions	11
3	Getting to Know Yourself through Purpose	18
4	Know Your Vision and Blueprint	30
5	Understanding the Importance of Decisions	40
6	What Holds You Back?	47
7	Spiritual Assets	53
8	The Map Begins with Thinking	73
9	Fear and Success	84
10	Gratitude Simplified	93
11	Balance	101
12	Belief and Faith	108
13	Determining Goals or Focus Points	114
14	Holding Space For What's To Come	122

15 The Art of Detachment · 131

16 Remembering and Awakening · 140

17 Separating Mind and Heart · 147

18 The Truth of it All · 153

19 Putting it Together · 161

About The Author · 177

About the Illustrator · 179

Unhinge Yourself: Embracing Your Authentic Medicine Through the Shamanic Wheel · 181

Preface

It has been 15 years since the day I tried to take my life at the age of 21. Life's chaos was overwhelming, difficult to unpack and understand. Anxiety clouded my soul, fueling life experiences that reinforced my belief that life no longer needed me. I know what it feels like to try solving everyone's problems but your own. I had neither the focus nor the energy to continue. At that point, I felt I had done everything I needed to, and it was time to go.

My puppy at the time was the only being who could stop me from committing suicide. Her 18 pounds of pure love burst through the door, frantically knocking the blade from my hand. She wagged her tail, jumping at my face until I looked at her. Her deep brown eyes transformed into swirls of love and compassion, a depth of love I couldn't comprehend at the time. Those swirls morphed into the black and purple hues of the cosmic sky. Lost in her gaze, I felt the embrace of the spirit enveloping us both, trickling into my heart with each heart-beat. Taking deep breaths, I began to cry uncontrollably as her muzzle nudged my face, seeking a hug. I scooped her into my arms and started to feel again. I began to breathe and awaken within my soul.

We all have stories—stories that lead us down dark tunnels of reality, leaving us questioning the purpose of those experiences. Life is chaos. Chaos provides opportunities to see what is right in front of us. My dog, Roxy, was a being contracted to awaken me when no one else could. My rebirth began that day—the journey of awakening my true nature. Awakening is why I am here in this life, but it didn't happen overnight; it continues to flow with each heart-led step I take. Each physical, mental, and emotional challenge has guided me closer to my core. I found my way back to my root medicine, the call screaming from my heart, urging me to align my mind back to my spirit. "Center yourself, Sarah," echoed from my core daily from that point forward.

My search began with mastering the mind. I believed the mind was my obstacle. I studied under teachers, masters, and mentors—from Carl Jung to new-age spirituality, Buddhism, and the Tao. I absorbed every motivational speaker I could find, seeking an answer to the silent call. How could I gain mastery over my mind? My morning walks with Roxy were the most peaceful moments before the daily quests began. I missed a critical step, but it was never far away.

My root medicine led me to my heart—a unique reset that helped me define my place in this modern world. I was able to remap my mind to create space for healing, learning, processing, and reaffirming our greatest human assets. I studied with Shamans for over eight years, only to realize that everything I had done, explored, and researched in my life pointed back to the foundational medicine in humanity. This is what Mystics, Sages, Masters, and Gurus discuss: we must clear the mind to allow the heart to emerge, the spirit of all. The process began to click together like dominoes.

As I sat in front of my computer, the map flowed out faster than I could type. Imagine a tree. We don't see its roots, but without strong, solid roots, the tree couldn't withstand the elements. Over time, the trunk thickens as its branches support the leaves reaching for the sun, which nourishes the roots below. Similarly, envision yourself as a tree. Your roots are unseen, dark, and deeply embedded within the Earth, yet you always receive exactly what you need at any given moment— not what we want, but what we need—to grow a robust trunk and branches capable of supporting leaves and flowers. We must always acknowledge the health of our roots.

Mind Spirit Mapping is a guide to help you feel the roots and acknowledge the beautiful being you are. You are a being of dark and light, Heaven and Earth, space and stars. We put too much pressure on ourselves! This map is a life process that took me 28 years to clarify. I wrote this book in hopes that it will create clarity in your mind, so you may choose your heart through understanding and love. The answer is always love, but it becomes cliché if we do not empty our minds and open our hearts. We keep it simple with questions designed to awaken your soul. An awakened heart and soul cannot unsee or not feel the truth of who you are, because that's all it knows.

Live Your Medicine,

Sarah Breen

June 3, 2022

About the Cover

Leslie Baker ~ Illustrator

"The cherry blossom tree stretches out her branches full of its sweet flowers. They pull at the skies of the heavens, soaking up the light through the shades of her pink. Candy for the eyes, she sways softly over Mother Earth. Her petals offering a dance of shade and sun as they flow with the wind. The divine feminine energy flows down to her roots that she digs deep, anchoring into the love of our world.

On the other side, sunflowers bask in the divine masculine glow of the sun. Their eyes devour the light of the warm rays, allowing them to grow strong in a cluster of golden glory. They work together in an intricate underground unity so that each flower can grow to reach its full shine.

Below, Mother Gaia opens her lands to reveal the beat of her heart, that flows in the perfect harmony of the in-between. The red heart of passion beating the rhythm of its energy through all of us. She shows us the way to our universe inside, waiting for us to explore the depths of who we are.

To help guide us through the deep waters, the magic of the whale and its sacred knowledge cradles the Earth. His eyes are led by the light of the feminine flow. Bringing what is kept in the caves of the unexplored oceans to the surface, so it can shine and grow in the sun.

As all of this works in its harmonized choreography, Mother Earth spreads her wings in freedom of unlocking who she authentically is. Dancing around her, the butterfly blesses her with the flutter of transformation. Her heart of passion is on fire, and everything is possible with this flame. It holds the key to unlock the door to remember. The key to our existence."

- Leslie Baker

Illustrator

Introduction

Welcome to The Earth School Guide to Mind Spirit Mapping™. This complete guide is designed to walk you through remapping your mind back to your spirit and heart with courage, grace, and understanding.

This channeled and meticulously crafted process will transition you from a state of confusion to a state of knowing and well-being, culminating in complete oneness with your unique purpose and mission. It is your responsibility to challenge your own beliefs while gaining the understanding necessary to transition from your current reality to a redesigned reality—one where you call the shots and dance with life as it was meant to be, free from illusions imposed by others, free to live the life you know is yours.

We understand that every belief, theory, religion, scientific study, spiritualism, ancient wisdom, and body of knowledge has pointed to a very similar concept: each person is unique, with distinct personality traits on the physical plane that do not define their true nature. Your true nature is something felt, not spoken in linguistic terms. It is a "coming home" feeling, a purpose flowing through you, an indescribable energy force, a truth that you can know on a fundamental level.

After each chapter, you will have the opportunity to explore the Mind Spirit Mapping™ process in a visual and open-ended manner. The best way to decipher the mind is by allowing yourself to see the truth behind what you write. Be open and honest with yourself, and keep this book or notebook with you, as many seeds will be planted with the questions asked. Record your observations as patterns emerge throughout this journey.

We must learn to trust ourselves without the influence of others' thoughts. This is a process of rediscovering who you are. It doesn't matter your age, the extent of your knowledge, the number of degrees you hold, or the breadth of your experiences—anyone can begin to see the real person inside. Please understand that avoiding questions to escape discomfort will not serve you. Our society has numbed us with distractions. We can easily spend hours scrolling through social media while sitting next to our partner without engaging in a potentially uncomfortable conversation. But we all know that comfort with discomfort is necessary until you see what it yields. Trust me when I say, going through this process is 100% WORTH IT. YOU are WORTH it!

Lastly, remember that courage needs fear! When I decided to finally write the complete edition of The Earth School Guide to Mind Spirit Mapping, I was filled with terror throughout the entire process, from editing to publication. We need a healthy amount of fear to desire change for the better. This idea itself awakens the lion or lioness within you. Remember, EVERYONE you view as courageous or brave also feels fear! So, stop comparing and start making the change you feel waiting to emerge inside you. BE the spirit that your soul calls to every moment.

1

What Happened?

"Your reality shatters when you ask the soul of you deeper questions." ~ Sarah Breen

" The mask of Mother Earth cracks open, she reveals the depth of the universe that lies within the core." ~ Leslie Baker

You may feel like you have lost your way, lost your purpose, lost who you are. Many situations, life experiences, people, and unexpected events occur in our lives that may or may not have been for our best, or so we believe. So, what really happened? You are DISCONNECTED! Unplugged... no power source... your gas light is on... and your battery is flashing red! It took years of events and life experiences, creating beliefs around the idea that it is acceptable to be completely disengaged from who you really are. Been there!

Life just seems to stop flowing and it feels more like walking through quicksand. Panic, anxiety, worry, and fear is a daily knock on the door in your mind. What would happen if ___ happened? What do I do about ____? What am I supposed to do with ___? The list goes on and on. So, what really happened to get you to this point? I began my search for the answers shortly after I decided not to take my own life one cold rainy September day.

Thoughts raced through my head... why am I here? Is this some kind of joke? Is life really just a rat race? What is the purpose of all of this?? I was driving myself mad looking for answers. I found countless books and motivational speakers that would hype me up, only to fall on my face months later. I even dug into ancient philosophy which left me with more questions than answers. But I admit to being someone who enjoys breaking things apart and putting them back together until it makes sense in the easiest way possible. I enjoyed stumping people with rhetorical questions and the never- ending whys until their eyes would roll in the backs of their heads. But... this is one journey that has taken me from high points, to low points, and dancing in between, for a long, long time.

So, what happened to get you here? You willingly followed someone else's bliss. You may have done it consciously or unconsciously, but, either way, you are right here, right now. So, step up to the plate and take a hard look at where you have been. You will immediately think of each situation you perceive has done you or your family wrong. It's ok. You must start somewhere. Now the next step... breathe in... breathe out... and let it go... for now!

You see, every action of energy disbursement has an immediate reaction or ripple effect placed upon it in our Earth realm. The effects of those ripples solely rely on your focus upon it. You got it! Your constant attention to something is causing those ripples to turn into waves. Don't get me wrong, waves are fun until you find the undertow, then you are in a world of trouble in seconds.

This word DISCONNECTED, it feels right, doesn't it? When you look in the mirror you have no idea who is looking back at you, SO, you call yourself your name, your job title, and your college degrees. But it doesn't tell you WHY you're disconnected. You are disconnected because you hold vibrational belief patterns (ripple effects) within you that do NOT match who you are at your core. PERIOD!

I am all about simplicity, and simple is what you will get. You may find it hard to swallow some of the concepts on these pages but my purpose in life is to translate the jargon into easy to understand answers. The box you have been living in your entire life looks like a fragment of energy from afar, a FRAGMENT of what you can be. I am not saying this from an ego standpoint... I am saying this because I love everyone for who they are, where they are, on their evolution to the center of themselves, which ultimately is the core of ALL! This may be hard to believe now but I can assure you the more you are willing to look at yourself, the more you will be able to control your outcomes.

Control?!?!?!? Yes, we love control! That is the main reason why people are so disconnected. Their focus is on controlling the outcome rather than WHAT to control in your daily life. So, yes, you will learn to control your life by finding the center of you first. Why are you here then? To be YOU fully and then EXPAND!

Why Am I Here?

We are here in a Earth School reality trying our best to remember our purpose through life experiences. Each life experience creates the opportunity for you to learn and evolve. To evolve we must remain open to challenging ourselves by asking questions. You may feel like these are silly questions but the simpler they are... the hard you find it to answer. The point of each question is for us to start to see where you are and where you want to be. Take each question seriously and go with your first response. If you need to read the questions in the morning, think about them during your day, and then answer them before bed then do it. If you want to run through them, answer them quick, and the reread them, then do that. There is no right or wrong way to do this besides taking them seriously.

Remember that the reason you may feel so disconnected is because you have either followed what someone else wanted from you or you are trying to control a situation from the wrong end. Take a good look at the questions below to help you uncover examples of yourself.

What major event or situation do you believe has you in an unwanted result?

____

____

____

____

____

____

____

____

Thinking back on this situation or event... has this type of pattern happened more than once? It may look different, but the result feels the same. If so, please explain.

____

____

____

____

____

____

____

____

What is the result you're trying to achieve? Describe what you feel and where you feel it in your body.

____

____

____

____

____

____

____

____

Now think back to the beginning when this idea of a desired result came to you; was this idea yours to begin with or an attempt to satisfy someone else? Please explain below.

2

Asking the Right Questions

"Release the burden of things you cannot control." ~ Sarah Breen

"Leading our path with the light of the North Star, we follow with faith in every step." ~ Leslie Baker

A valuable lesson in this process is learning to ask yourself the right questions. Asking why to every question is great as a child but as an adult, it can make a mountain out of a molehill. We are dedicated to giving you more than enough understanding on the topic of yourself, vibrational placement, and much more, so it will satisfy the "why" child inside of you. First, we must give ourselves permission to uncover who we really are. Now, you might find that statement strange but I can tell you from experience and teachings that people don't know how to give themselves permission. We had to ask to use the bathroom, ask our parents if we could use the car or go out with friends. Should I go on?

We filter and navigate life through verbal language instead of allowing ourselves to feel first. So, yes, you do have to go through the process of giving yourself permission to uncover YOU, because up to this point you have needed permission for basically everything in your life.

Next, release the burden of things you cannot control. This allows you to jump off the hamster wheel with the expectation of getting out of the cage at some point. How do you do it? By identifying what you do control, and that is ONLY YOU, not your spouse, child, boss, coworkers, friends, etc. You only control YOU and how you think, feel, and act. If you continually try to control others, you are destined to a lifetime of running on a hamster wheel. You won't get anywhere. Parents may have a different opinion. But mull this over; as a parent myself, the only thing I am responsible for is creating a safe and thriving environment for my children to grow and expand as we are all meant to do. Imagine a world where children grew up encouraged to fully be the core of themselves, day in and day out? They would never feel disconnected or have events in their lives like we have gone through ourselves. HOPE lies in the hands of our future; your job as a parent is to focus on expanding you, and your children will blossom just as fast, if not faster than you could ever imagine.

In any situation in which you dislike the outcome, begin to ask yourself questions like:

What does this mean to me?

What was the prominent feeling in this situation?

What would I want to feel instead?

Notice there are no HOW or WHY questions in there? They all start with WHAT. A what question makes you think about you in the situation. It makes you think deeper to uncover what really matters in the situation. What matters most is how you feel. If you feel miserable more than joyful, this is the greatest indicator of your disconnection. You can't experience your center in a state of misery, like a child having a temper tantrum; your center is a soft nudge, a gentle feeling, that you experience when in a calm state.

Starting today, begin to take responsibility for everything that has happened to you, and everything you are creating. You have created the world around you, both consciously and unconsciously. You may not like hearing it but everything that has happened has served a purpose in your evolving life. It has served its purpose in the evolution of your journey. Taking responsibility for your own thoughts, feelings, actions, and reactions will serve you in learning to listen to the core of you. Your focus should be that which we are all striving for and achieving each day: full enjoyment of the present and ever- expanding abundance. Focus on finding your core truth and invite it in.

Our world is evolving at an unprecedented rate. Not in a bad way, in a good way in terms of mass consciousness. Because of people like you, our future is so much brighter. I believe the reason our species is still here on this planet is because we choose to ask the right questions and, because we always receive an answer, we will continue to evolve faster than ever before. So brace yourself and do not be afraid of uncovering your truth. Do not be afraid as it will meet you like a welcome home surprise party. You are so loved on so many levels, dimensions, and realms. You are never alone on this journey, for those who fight your evolution process are those who will be the final stragglers in the push for dimensional uplifting. Call it what you want, words are only words, but you will understand it as you journey to the center of your core, your spirit, your full truth.

What are the Right Questions?

We now must address giving yourself permission. Writing things out one tool and speaking it out loud in the mirror is the second step in this process. Please rewrite the below statement and repeat it in the mirror while looking at yourself till you feel you have made the point to yourself. Sounds funny but try it.

Statement:

"I _______ (your name) give myself permission to go beyond my limited thinking and discover what I am really made of no matter what my mind tells me; I am walking forward TODAY!"

____

____

____

____

____

____

____

Recall and explain a situation you recently experienced that left you feeling disempowered, angry, confused, etc. Explain below.

____

____

____

____

____

____

Now using that situation as your example ask the Right Question: What does this mean to me?

What is the prominent feeling in this situation?

____
____

What would I want to feel instead?

____
____
____
____
____
____
____
____
____

What in the situation do you have control over?

____
____
____
____
____
____
____
____
____

These questions might sound funny at first but before you know it, you will be asking yourself these question BEFORE your feelings take you on a ride down the rabbit hole. It takes practice and willingness on your part to start to analyze where your mind is taking you. This is the part of the map that will make you laugh, cry, and want to scream into pillow at the same time. Life is growth… you have to start here.

3

Getting to Know Yourself through Purpose

"The key to life is realizing and choosing to organizing chaos into reality."
~ Sarah Breen

"A door to the fulfillment of our hearts awaits to be unlocked by the key that holds our true passions." ~ Leslie Baker

If you feel like your life isn't working out, or you're walking in circles, then this is a sign that you are not listening to your core, your heart, or living with purpose.

You may feel numb, overwhelmed, exhausted, or even downright confused when you have a moment to sit with your thoughts.

Without a purpose consciously identified, you will feel like life is happening to you, not for you. We are all on the same path in life... But what you DO on that path is individual and specific to your purpose. That is what makes us the expanding beings we are.

In fact, it's the largest factor that separates us from animals. We have a reasoning MIND that allows us to CHOOSE what we DO on our path, on our journey to a life full of purpose.

Take a moment to hear this warning: if you do not take the efforts to discover and live your purpose, then much of your life will be spent running in circles, putting out fires, and living this life of struggle that the mainstream identifies as normal.

But you - yes, you - you had a flame that lit up inside you that told you, "there is something more than what you see today." And you're absolutely right... Your life has a purpose! That is what we are here to discover.

Now, this isn't something you come to a complete realization of overnight. This is a process of discovery. I challenge you today to take the first steps to uncover your purpose.

Your purpose is your WHY. This is WHO YOU ARE. Your purpose serves as a lifeline you hold to your heart. It helps you form beliefs, decisions, actions, and, ultimately, the results you achieve. So yes, this is a critical piece of the puzzle we call LIFE. You may think this is a difficult task at first so please be gentle with yourself. You can choose to stare at a mountain from afar, or you can choose to walk towards it.

You do not have to accept these ideas but I ask you to not ignore them completely either. Understand that we are all creative beings with the ability to create anything we want in our lives if it matches our core purpose, beliefs, and intentions. That is what you are here to learn and apply to create a well-rounded life, full of everything you can imagine.

We create our lives moment by moment in the creative fields of our minds and heart. But to live the results you want... we must begin by living and leading with your purpose, your heart center.

In your mind, build the foundation that will hold the map for the life you will create from here on out. Discovering your purpose gives you the direction you desire. It's an inner calling that drives all the forces you need to acquire all that you are. There is something in your life that you love doing. Keep thoughts of, "well, I can't see how I can make money doing that," at bay. Those ideas will keep you living the same results over and over.

Fall in love with your center. What is love? It is an energy felt in your heart that can be reflected outside of you in terms of appreciation. This energy equates to a feeling. We want you to fall in love with those things that make you feel alive, excited, fulfilled, appreciative, and whole. When this happens it means that your mind and spirit have reconnected. When you start to find your purpose, IT GUIDES YOU. You begin to see the synchronicities in life–chance meetings and conversations that help you consciously identify your purpose. No control is needed, you need only follow and listen. Any action you think you need to take will be felt through your heart, not your mind.

Acting from the heart is acting with purpose and intention. It sparks your inner child and the possibilities begin to appear. It ignites your imagination. You start acting with PURPOSE, desire, and love. You compose your own symphony when you start living from your heart.

Here is a warning... know that negative ideas and experiences have been bombarding our existence since the day we were born. From trying to fit in, to red marks on tests, you have a conscious awareness of all the negativity and failures in life. That is exactly what has shut your heart down and keeps you from listening to it. Let's face it, the masses are afraid of change, so they decide to conform instead. They would rather keep things the same than express the unique, creative abilities of each individual. You must acknowledge the uniqueness you hold inside yourself.

When you focus on the mysteries of yourself, you will ignite the flames of opportunity. The spaces open up in your mind and spirit to align with opportunities you otherwise would have missed before. You begin to see the shifting around you and your thoughts. Things begin to show up to amplify who you really are. Like attracts like... therefore you will attract what is dominant in your mind and then what is in your spirit. Make sure you are asking yourself the right questions.

Purpose gives meaning to WHY you are doing what you're doing. You don't need to justify it to anyone else. It's time to listen to that inner voice. That is what this is all about! Your inner voice will never steer you wrong! You must give serious attention to what comes naturally to you. We think our paths in life should be hard instead of allowing our natural gifts to shine through. We take for granted what comes naturally to us without acknowledging that it's our hearts guiding us. Mull that over for a minute and feel a different force awaken within you.

You are NOT on this planet to live someone else's dream but to create your own! Walking a path not consciously designed by you will never bring you happiness because it was never yours to begin with. Determining your purpose is an internal process of taking responsibility for reconnecting to your heart; you cannot expect your family and friends to answer questions only your heart knows the answers to.

Resentment is born from situations like that. When you believe you have found your purpose...DO NOT allow yourself to be persuaded differently by others. Do not allow them to tell you how you should build or in which direction. I suggest keeping it to yourself and allow your imagination to take the lead. Start by asking yourself the right questions to uncover the mysteries inside of you, the things that make you tick.

Here are some questions to ask yourself:

- What accomplishments have you achieved?
- What makes you different from others?
- What creative ideas repeat often in your mind?
- What characteristics do you hold inside of you?
- What comes naturally to you?
- What sparks your interest?
- What do you value the most?
- What do you love to do in your free time?
- What activities do you participate in that seem to make you lose track of time?
- What experiences have given you the opportunity to grow?

Notice that when you are answering some of these questions they are mostly, if not all, creatively based. These questions are simple but will take some time to digest. We as humans overcomplicate everything in our lives because we must know the answers to everything. Don't compare yourself to others. Every heart is unique and beats to its' own drum. If you find yourself focusing on others, take some deep breaths and refocus your thoughts on all the good that is inside you.

Life is simple and creative! You can either accept that idea or reject it. Either way, your results will show it.

This is your starting point. You must know where you are on the map in order to get where you want to be. Take a moment and breathe. Note that all that has been presented in your life has prepared you for this moment. This is a new day, a new opportunity, a pushpin on a map with a string to your next destination. This is a journey of life fulfillment in ALL areas of your life. Consider the above questions carefully as they are the key to unlocking your heart on this journey.

Living with Purpose

To begin to rediscover ourselves we must understand what makes us tick. Using the questions below, explore your past in a non-judgmental manner of the situation. Only focus on your feelings. How? By feeling your heart in this process. You may feel excited about the memory as it comes up from the depths of your mind, or you may cry tears of joy. This is a FEEL-GOOD exercise so please use this time to pat yourself on the back and see the good qualities about yourself.

What accomplishments have you achieved that makes you the proudest?

____

____

____

____

____

____

____

What do YOU feel makes you unique?

What creative ideas repeat in your head often?

What characteristics do you hold inside of you that you do with ease?

____

____

____

____

____

____

____

____

What comes naturally to you?

____

____

____

____

____

____

____

____

What are some things that spark your interest?

____

____

____

____

____

____

____

____

____

What do you value the most in yourself?

____

____

____

____

____

____

____

____

What do you LOVE to do in your free time and why?

____

____

____

____

____

____

____

____

What activities do you participate in that you seem to lose track of time?

____

____

____

____

____

____

____

____

What experiences have given you the opportunity to grow?

____

____

____

____

____

____

____

____

Now look back at all of your answers and start to get a gauge of what you LOVE about yourself. These are the unique qualities that you cannot seem to understand why they aren't important to others, because they ARE so important to you. These are the shiny flags of your spirit that you are looking for in discovering your unique purpose. It's like driving a car and getting aggravated because no one likes to use their blinker. Guess what... you're the driver and YOU ARE the one not using the blinker. This questioning process gets you to STOP, THINK, and FEEL. Who cares about what other people see you as? What is important is what YOU feel. PERIOD.

Now take the time to write down how you really feel about yourself based on the answers you gave in this discovery process. Note the patterns and areas of focus. Do not overthink this. Just write.

____

____

____

____

____

____

____

____

____

____

____

____

____

____

____

____

____

____

Now re-read what you have written. Take a moment and see the patterns of your feelings. This is your spirit trying to speak through the cracks of your overactive mind. Come back to this often as the more you allow yourself to feel, the more you will experience in the outside world to mirror what your purpose is. This isn't an activity of the mind, instead it's an activity to start listening to the heart and discarding the mind.

4

Know Your Vision and Blueprint

"The mind does not know it is a being of infinite potential"
~ Sarah Breen

"Once a caterpillar seeing the sky from the grounds below, the soul
of the butterfly now flies with the winds above." ~ Leslie Baker

Now that we know where you are, it's time to make a conscious choice about where you want to go. Most people, when asked what they want in life, will give answers like, "I want a million dollars!" or "I just want to be free!" These responses are valid and should not be disregarded. However, if you sit with the simple question, "What do you want?" your head may begin to spin, or you might not even know where to begin.

Keep this idea in the back of your mind as you continue with this process: understand that nothing is ever permanent, and everything is always changing. With that perspective, let's gain a greater understanding of visioneering and its importance in your life.

As a small child, you had a natural grasp of imagination. Clouds became your playhouse, and the grass you lay on became your audience. Your mind is the most impressive tool you can utilize to regain your cellular memory of imagination. In fact, without the use of your imagination, your life would not be what it is today, for better or worse. Consider this: if you've ever said to yourself, "I knew that would turn out like that," you used your imagination to create that reality.

Now, I may have struck a chord, so I'll say it again: you utilize your imagination every day to create your reality, moment by moment. Life is an illusion created in your mind. If life hasn't gone the way you planned, it's okay to admit that you have been imagining in the "I don't want that to happen" direction.

Consciously understanding yourself—mind, body, and spirit—will lead you to develop your thoughts, feelings, and responses in an enlightened manner, guiding you to the wholeness that is uniquely yours.

Let's turn your attention to desire. Desire begins with a vision, which is coupled with a purpose, and your purpose is the guiding force in your life. Your desires can range from feelings to material possessions, but know that every desire ultimately equates to a feeling that links to your core values. The key to creating your vision is to give yourself permission to think wildly and freely. Avoid the "yeah, buts," the "how am I going to do this?" and the "Let's be realistic." Go wild and make a decision to begin this process of thinking outside the box.

Once you begin the imagination process, the vision itself needs to be flexible. We live in a world that often sees things in black and white, with no room for gray. We are programmed to think that flexibility means chaos and lack of structure. As you journey through this process and really dive into the nuts and bolts of who you are, you will begin to rediscover parts of yourself that have been missing for a very long time. That realization alone can be incredibly freeing.

I am not here to tell you what your vision should be; I am here to guide and prod your mind to reunite with the essence, the spirit, of you. Words never teach; your experiences do. Therefore, it is your job to exercise your mind to reconnect yourself back to your TRUTH. I state this with confidence because this is how this process has been exercised for centuries, starting with the indigenous people of our time. Back then, they had silence, solitude, and life without a clock. Today, we are surrounded by noise and social media, and time feels like it's running out day by day. It is your time now to regain your balance and walk the path that calls to you every moment of every day.

Exercising your imagination is a gentle process, one that requires you to set aside demands or time-frames that create stress and force. Begin when your state of mind is at ease and relaxed. Carve out time for yourself to create a space to relax and allow your mind to explore your desires. This is the process of rediscovering who you really are. In doing so, you recommit to the promises you made to yourself and will release thoughts of unworthiness, those feelings that have broken your spirit time and again.

You may begin by identifying your needs. As you write down your needs, pay special attention to where they are coming from. Are they stemming from lack and limitation, or are they emerging from a deep, loving desire from within? You will begin to feel the difference as you continue to write. Your needs will transform into wants, and your wants into a vision. One final step in this process is staying true to your values. By identifying your core values, you begin to see patterns in your desires and visions. Are they in alignment with your own truth? If we operate outside of our core values, no matter how much energy we put into something, it will never turn out the way we want. Theology suggests that rejection is God's protection.

Identifying your core values is not a step you want to skip. It helps you determine what is most important to you and what uniquely drives you; it grounds and aligns you with who you really are and helps you understand how and why you tick.

It's time to step into your vision. It's time to walk the path that you create. It's time to live by your own design because that is the journey we are meant to experience.

To know yourself on a more intimate level, we must acknowledge that each person has a unique set of values for their journey, purpose, mission, and values that they discover in this human experience. Getting to know what you value the most will help you understand which experiences align with you and what you can give yourself permission to let fall away. Getting to know yourself in this manner ensures that things will work out better than you could have imagined because you are working closer to the spirit inside who lives and breathes within your DNA.

Core Values Exercise

Step 1: Brainstorm Your Key Values

Start with taking the list below and quickly circle the words that jump out at you. Do not overthink this process as we need to have your gut tell us what is most important to you. These words help you feel something at your core. Simply circle as many words as you feel needed. This is a general list and you may add any words to it that you feel are personally important to you.

Abundance	Family	Effectiveness
Awareness	Flexibility	Enjoyment
Ambition	Fun	Expressiveness
Affection	Generosity	Fairness
Beauty	Growth	Focus
Calmness	Accountability	Friendship
Community	Achievement	Grace
Compassion	Accomplishment	Happiness
Collaboration	Appreciation	Acceptance
Creativity	Boldness	Advancement
Credibility	Caring	Adventure
Dedication	Commitment	Balance
Determination	Confidence	Brilliance
Discipline	Consciousness	Challenge
Empathy	Curiosity	Charity
Enthusiasm	Daring	Connection
Excellence	Dignity	Contribution
Consistency	Decisiveness	Courage

Courtesy
Dependability
Discovery
Drive
Energy
Ethical
Experience
Fearless
Freedom
Giving
Gratitude
Hard Work
Health
Humility
Integrity
Inspiring
Kindness
Learning

Liberty
Mindfulness
Mastery
Order
Organization
Peace
Prosperity
Quality
Respect
Resourcefulness
Resilient
Spirituality
Silence
Serenity
Success
Teamwork
Tranquility
Honesty

Harmony
Intuitive
Justice
Knowledge
Leadership
Logic
Moderation
Meaning
Optimism
Open-Minded
Performance
Purpose
Reason
Reflective
Responsibility
Service
Simplicity
Skillfulness

Sensitivity
Support
Thoughtfulness
Truth
Humor
Intimacy
Intelligence
Joy
Love
Loyalty
Making a Difference
Motivation
Openness
Originality
Passion
Personal Development

Professionalism
Recognition
Reliability
Risk
Sharing
Security
Stability
Structure
Talent
Trustworthiness
Traditional
Uniqueness
Unity
Valor
Warmth
Usefulness

Vision
Versatility
Wealth
Understanding
Victory
Well-Being
Wisdom

Step 2: Group Your Values

Next, take your list of circled words and begin to group similar words together into categories. Create up to five main groups. Base your grouping solely on what makes the most sense to you.

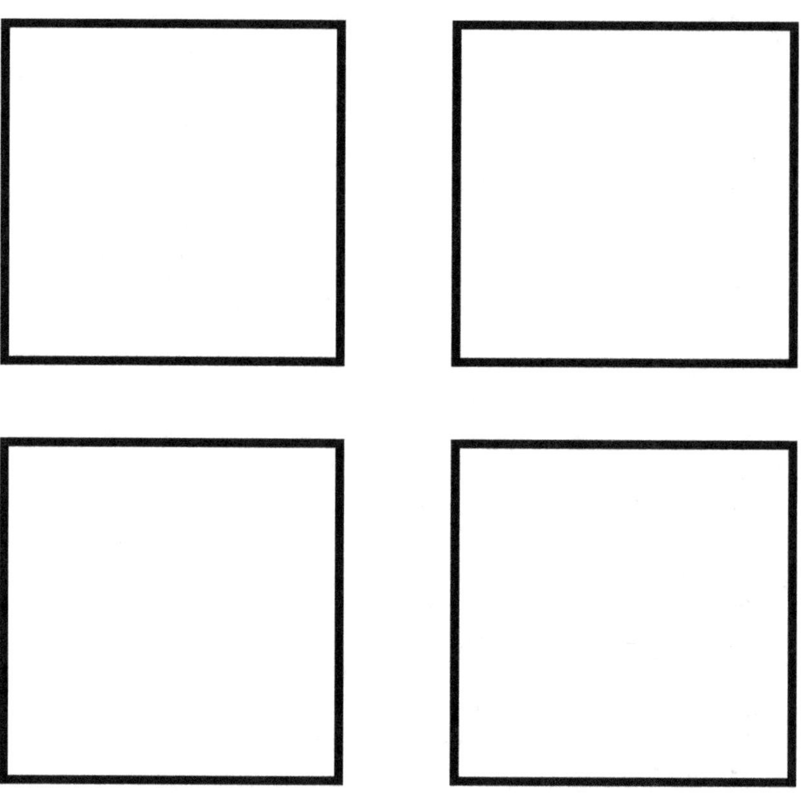

Step 3: Identify Your Groups

Go back to Step 2 and choose one value from each group that you feel best describes that entire section using that to label your group. Please do not overthink or analyze this part. When reaching for this value you will create all that is explained within that group. Each value describes the meaning of your main choice in each section. Have fun with this!

Step 4: Write them out

Now with your top five values write a sentence out for each one stating why it is important to you using some of the words within groups to help describe it to you. This is how your values will become a new perspective for you.

Value 1: ____

____

____

____

____

____

Value 2: ____

____

____

____

____

____

Value 3: ____

____

____

____

____

____

Value 4: ____

____

____

____

____

Value 5: ____

____

____

____

____

____

5

Understanding the Importance of Decisions

"The journey is about following the call within your soul." ~ Sarah Breen

"Swimming from the depths of our subconscious, a whale honors our song of truth." ~ Leslie Baker

"Decisions, decisions, decisions..." This phrase often leads to indecision. Just the thought of making a decision can send your mind into a loop. "What do you want to eat?" "I don't know, what do you feel like?" We can all relate to this conversation, having experienced it many times.

Decision-making is a fundamental skill that you need to reteach yourself. You heard that right—reteach yourself how to make decisions. You make decisions all day long in business, family, and social settings, but when it comes to making decisions that align with who you really are, you may find yourself with more questions than answers, making it difficult to reach a resolution.

What does the word 'decision' mean? According to the dictionary, it is "a conclusion or resolution reached after consideration." Yet, many people suffer from procrastination, which is defined as "the action of delaying or postponing something."

So, after careful consideration, we have concluded that the cure for procrastination is—let's hear it—DECISION! You may smirk at these simple definitions, but the conscious repetition of understanding the simplicity will help you more than you realize. When you neglect to make an evolving decision, you carve deeper grooves into your mind that keep you stuck in a rut: the same actions create the same results. It's like pressing play on a familiar song and expecting to hear something different.

The next question we often hear is, "How do I know I am making the right decision?" This is a very important question when you are starting out because we have made many decisions in the past that may not have created the results we intended.

This brings us to what this entire journey is about. It's about learning to make evolutionary decisions by listening to the inner voice, your intuition, that has been there since you were a child. It is my goal to give you the tools you need to become who you intended to be at birth. Through all the experiences in my life, I embraced the idea that I thought differently than others. I would pick up a situation and look at all angles, all sides, and way beyond the box to seek what felt right. I had the privilege as a child to have a mother who encouraged me to embrace my individuality and experience life as I saw fit creatively. Of course, my mother created the safest space possible for me to do so, and those moments growing up, making decisions by following my feelings, led me to be able to guide you through what really works.

Your decisions must come from the core of you. As you walk through this process, there is a key question you must ask yourself: "Is this a step towards my desire?" In other words, "Does it feel good to go this way, or does it feel uncomfortable and lead me away from my desire?" Then, you must listen to the first response your core gives you. It is usually a quick yes or no, but sometimes you get a pause or maybe nothing. Often, a core response will present as an expansion or opening in your heart area (yes!) or a constriction in your upper torso where your shoulders hunch forward, and a weight settles into your chest (no!). Sometimes, a yes will feel like pure joy and excitement, while a no might make your stomach clench or feel nauseous. All these responses are normal while you learn to take cues from your core. Pay attention to the first response only; anything beyond that will lead to overthinking, causing doubt, resentment, guilt, or fear. If the pause happens, put the question aside and return to it within twenty-four hours.

The purpose of this simple question is to help you gain confidence that you hold the answer inside. Ultimately, you're reigniting the belief in yourself that you had all along. We live in an action-oriented world; we think nothing will get done unless we do it ourselves, and we have forgotten how to pause and move from our core. Living in a busy, noisy world, there is a gap in modern-day personal growth. That gap is holding space for the most powerful part of you to thrive. Many self-help books and spiritual teachings discuss an invisible force that operates the larger part of you. Most people agree that we are a shell that embodies energy to experience this life on both a spiritual and physical level.

So, what does this have to do with decisions? Decide today to explore the largest part of you, to use that creative side constructively and humbly to achieve well-being in terms of balance, harmony, and happiness in every area of your life. The remaining part of you is your free will. You have the ability to choose to embrace it or numb it further. I'm choosing right now to create balance and harmony by centering my higher self, providing you the tools to assist you, and watching you soar. It's your decision. Will you choose to take the leap?

Decisions

Revisiting the skill of decision-making is crucial. Take the questions below and apply them to a decision you have been avoiding. If you don't have a current decision, use one you made in the past and put yourself back into that scenario for this exercise.

How would I feel if I did not decide?

____

____

____

____

____

How would I feel if I tried?

____

____

____

____

____

What does my gut tell me about this situation?

Do I feel like I would grow from this situation?

Will it be a steppingstone to my next desire?

What do I have to lose?

The question "What do I have to lose?" may send you on a loop of rhetorical questioning, but understand that everything you see, feel, smell, taste, and touch is made from a frequency that belongs solely to the universe. In the end, you have nothing to lose because we are living in a frequency-based universe. The more you try to hold onto something in an ever-changing universe, the further it will slip away from you, since everything is in constant motion.

If I am to achieve the desired feeling I have specified in my life, how will I **DECIDE** TODAY to LIVE everyday moving forward? What would that look, feel, and be like? Describe below.

6

What Holds You Back?

"The roots create the tree of beauty and grace." ~ *Sarah Breen*

"Sweet blossoms bloom for their moment of glory in the light, shining bright the uniqueness of their own radiance." ~ *Leslie Baker*

So far, we have discussed your purpose, the process of reigniting your imagination, and what the decision-making process should look like. Now, it's time to address the purple elephant in the room: the blocks!

You may or may not have heard the term "paradigm." For our purposes, a paradigm can be defined as a pattern of thought that keeps repeating in your mind; it ultimately turns into a belief that may or may not be true to the core of you. Essentially, a paradigm is a belief in your mind that shapes your results and the reality you experience.

How do you release the blocks, those stepping stones that lead to less than satisfactory results? Change the paradigm or belief about the idea, and your results will change with it. That's easier said than done because you have an entire lifetime of experiences that have created your belief or judgment about a situation.

To break through these blocks, we must always remain curious. Every thought, reaction, and conclusion we have in our lives is created by a dominant thought pattern in our minds. To remain curious is to begin using the simple question we discussed in the previous section: "Is this a step towards my desire, or does it lead me away from it?"

By starting this process of questioning your beliefs, how things should work out, or why you do the things you do when you know you should be doing something else, you will find a pattern in your thinking. Your job is to find a common thread throughout these thoughts. Could this be stemming from an idea of lack, feeling unworthy, or just plain fear? The threads might connect back to intricately knit ideas. Notice how those threads are completely opposite to what you value the most in your life. Notice how you feel when you speak out loud to yourself. Now, observe how these threads weave through your experiences and affect the pattern every time you approach something new.

With enough understanding of a paradigm, you can begin to challenge those ideas and conclude the truth about them. This isn't a small task by any means and is completely part of your journey day in and day out. Each experience, situation, and chance meeting will give you the unique opportunity to uncover those patterns and create a new pattern moving forward. What we are really talking about here is a practice of centering your emotions and then moving them in a direction that matters the most to you; your core. Your paradigms create your habits. You may have a habit of reacting a certain way about relationships, money, your job, or even other people's success. Identifying your core values will create the map leading to your true core.

Your blocks are your conditioned way of thinking on autopilot. Until you become conscious of your automatic choices and reactions, your results will never change. Taking this one step further, where your focus goes (consciously or unconsciously) your results will always show.

How do you change your results?

By working on the creative side of you—your spiritual assets, the side of you that has been buried and locked in a box. You know the box is there, but did you know you hold the key to unlock it? Through the process of Mind Spirit Mapping™, you will unlock your spiritual assets and operate with a full understanding of how the game of life works. On a side note, please understand that you are programmed to think in sequential processes. But each individual person has his or her own process or spiral in life that is unique to his or her own unfolding. You will begin to see the purpose of all this when you are willing and open to your own journey.

Starting today, remain aware of your results to date. This is not a time to dredge up old memories or place blame. This is a time to slow the freight train down by asking yourself, "What did that mean to me?" Slowly, one by one, each rock-hard, stubborn block will begin to soften, and you will anchor your emotions to a neutral point where you can do some core work.

Before you move on and work with your spiritual assets, be aware of where your paradigms show their ugly faces. Begin by pondering this question:

In what ways do you feel life has been unfair?

This will give you a starting point. Remain curious and realize that your emotions can easily cloud your judgment if you allow them to.

The more you practice remaining open and neutral, the easier it will become to dictate the outcome of that emotional focal point.

Answering the question will create fertile ground into which you can plant seeds. When a seed starts to sprout, the dirt comes up with it as it reaches towards the sun, but the goal is continual positive growth. The dirt, or paradigms, must come up! This means, if you're willing to face your decisions in a centered manner, you can focus on your journey. That is the true nature of manifestation.

The Blocks

Those blocks always seem to get in the way. In fact, by merely acknowledging that you're blocked, you solidify their presence. From this point on, stop using them as an unconscious crutch. Make a conscious decision to tear down what you perceive as blocks. How? By beginning to notice the patterns and gaining a new perspective to turn them around. Slow down the freight train enough to neutralize the feeling, then move yourself into a new feeling closer to your heart. Start by asking yourself these simple, yet challenging, questions.

In what ways do you feel life has been unfair?

____

____

____

____

____

____

Does life seem to happen to you or for you? Why?

What are the common outcomes that seem to happen?

7

Spiritual Assets

"Work together within oneself creates the ability to embrace all of life's beauty." ~ Sarah Breen

"The synchronized dance of the butterfly wings, calls in the magic of revealing our soul's voice." ~ Leslie Baker

We will break down spiritual assets into creative tools. You can master any situation once you learn how to utilize these tools: Reason, Will, Memory, and Perception, which reside in your mind, along with Imagination and Intuition, which are rooted in your spirit. These are innate tools you were born with, actively used in childhood, and then gradually suppressed as you were pressured to conform.

As a child, your world centered around you. Your days were filled with play, fun, and joy. Granted, not every moment was filled with pure joy for everyone, but those moments of complete enjoyment and appreciation were far more potent than the negative thoughts imposed on you by others. Yes, you heard that correctly: negative thoughts—other people's paradigms—were introduced into your mind in an attempt to prevent harm or behavior that didn't fit communal standards. Although these actions were often taken in your best interest according to someone else's boundaries, something inside you recognized that they weren't true to your core.

I was a natural challenger. I believe my mother turned gray the moment I took my first steps. Challenging norms was my role, and I continue to embrace it daily as a means of growth. By 'challenge,' I don't mean engaging in conflict, but rather questioning everything with curiosity and independence. When I reawakened my spiritual assets as an adult, I quickly realized that my internal feelings had always been my truth. I was finally coming home. My core was softly speaking to me. And guess what—it felt incredible to recognize those gentle nudges and follow them without fear or doubt. I am offering you a glimpse into your future, a future where you are in control and witness your life flourish. This transformation is facilitated through your spiritual assets, grounded in the highest intentions for good, and fueled by a deep understanding that your joy and happiness are paramount.

A common question we encounter is, "Am I being selfish by focusing on my own happiness?" I encourage you to explore this question for yourself. Reflect on how we are conditioned to prioritize the needs of others above our own. Consider the safety instructions given before a flight: "Always put the oxygen mask on yourself first before helping others." How can you assist others if you are struggling to breathe yourself? The next time you hesitate to focus on your own emotions and happiness, observe the impact it has on those around you as they see you repeatedly experience the same outcomes, not living true to your core. As you progress on this journey, you will notice that by addressing your own thought patterns, you will initiate changes that ripple through past, present, and future generations. By improving yourself, you can influence generations with a single change in your pattern, breaking a cycle, catching a glimpse of your core truth. Those around you may not understand what you are doing, but they can feel it on a level beyond words. If you're not ready to fully embrace this concept now, simply consider it briefly, then let it go.

Reason

Let's discuss the first spiritual asset: your ability to reason. By definition, reason is "the action of thinking about something in a logical, sensible way." However, what constitutes a logical way? The definition of logical is "natural or sensible given the circumstances." Things deemed sensible or logical are simply ideas agreed upon after consideration. Thus, your ability to reason is entirely based on your beliefs and experiences. What is normal? What is logical? You create your own logic, your own normalcy, your own beliefs, though you may not have been told that you possess the authority to do so. Understand that each individual, culture, business, and society develops its own values, which in turn shape their logical beliefs and, consequently, their reasoning abilities. These groups create their own rules aligned with their values, which forge their logic and capacity to reason or think innovatively. This explains why individuals or businesses react strongly when their values are challenged.

Reason allows you to determine if something is in your best interest. Deciding whether an idea will benefit or harm you relies entirely on your logical thinking and beliefs. If you're unsure whether something serves your best interest, you then engage your other spiritual assets to find the most suitable response.

Children perceive new situations with fresh, innocent eyes. They inherently understand that the world is a magical playground where they can create and do what they desire, all in pursuit of joy. Your role is not to suppress their ability to reason but to learn from it. Protect them without instilling fear, teaching them about humanity without dampening their spirits with rigid paradigms and "logic."

My oldest child can reason through any situation and fully embrace his true core. I am captivated by his thought process, which allows him to flourish into a beacon of pure love and joy. Many of us need to reset our ability to reason, and observing children can help us reconnect with our inner child.

Will

The definition of will is "a deliberate or fixed desire or intention." This is your ACTION spiritual asset, an essential component of your core. Your will represents your ability to focus. For some, focusing is effortless, while others may find it challenging. For instance, some people excel in maintaining a meditative state, finding tranquility in stillness, whereas others struggle to quiet their minds long enough to achieve this. Both experiences are completely normal. It's important to understand that strengthening your will through practice makes it easier to connect with your spiritual assets.

Please do not confuse will with willpower. Often, when we discuss will, the term willpower comes to mind, which involves forcing oneself to avoid certain actions based on a goal. However, will is not about exertion; it is about embracing a new way of being. Your will is the ABILITY to maintain your reasoned decisions in your consciousness until they become in sync with your heart. Using force is unnecessary and can actually be counterproductive, as it might conflict with your core values.

Your will aids in focusing on what truly matters to you. It helps maintain your truth throughout your journey and distinguishes your authentic self from external influences. Your will enables you to prioritize your heart over your ego and to perceive the true essence of things around you. It acts as an inner guide, encouraging you to maintain those feelings, thoughts, or images in your heart. Ultimately, it assists you in finding your way back home.

Memory

Memory is often lamented with the phrase, "I have a terrible memory!"—a common misconception. Unfortunately, we often equate memory with the rote memorization required in school, overlooking its potential as a profound spiritual asset. Memorization involves storing knowledge temporarily for specific purposes, like schoolwork or directions.

Memory, defined as "the faculty by which the mind stores and recalls information," highlights the mind's role distinctly separate from the brain. To clarify, the mind is an energy force permeating every cell of your body, whereas the brain is a physical organ responsible for keeping the body functioning; it manages involuntary actions like breathing and blinking, operating like a communication highway to avert physical danger.

Both the mind and brain possess forms of memory. The brain handles conditioned memory—for example, if you touch something hot as a child, your nervous system's immediate reaction, "HOT! BACK AWAY!", imprints a conditioned response in your brain to avoid future harm. The brain stores myriad such responses to protect and sustain life.

Conversely, the mind traverses the energy spaces within and beyond your body. It harbors information potentially unknown to you, such as data from past lives, ancestral knowledge, and conditioned responses unlinked to experiences in your current lifetime. These imprints from various energy experiences are personally tied to you through the consciousness of your energy field. When connected to your spirit, your mind unveils the core truths about who you are. Tapping into this perfect spiritual memory is essential for your evolutionary journey.

You may choose to accept or disregard this information, and that's perfectly acceptable as we are all navigating this path together. Remember, your memory extends far beyond simple recall of names and addresses; it delves deeper, guiding your evolution as you reconnect your mind with your spirit. Whether you refer to this connection as God, Ether, Source, Universe, Angels, or Guides, choose the language that best helps you grasp the concept. Avoid getting entangled in the semantics, as words are merely tools to express feelings. Rest assured, we embrace you regardless of the terms you use to describe the expansive memory residing within your energetic field.

Perception

It is in perfect alignment to talk about the next spiritual asset of Perception. Perception is your ability to view your world in multidimensional ways and form insight you otherwise would have overlooked through your conventional program of logical thinking. It can be defined as *"the state of being or process of becoming aware of something through the senses."* Conventionally, you would perceive something through your physical senses; see, hear, smell, taste, touch; and not your energetic senses. Your energetic senses are what we are talking about now with your spiritual assets. Each asset goes hand in hand with your evolution up the spiral of life. What would you do in someone else's physical shoes? How would you know how their life experiences would dictate how they would respond in any situation? You don't unless you exercise your perception within the energetic field.

Taking perception a step further will give you a glimpse into what we are propelling you forward into. Utilizing perception only within a neutral state of being will grant you access into a heart-centered motion of compassion and understanding on a multi-dimensional level. What are dimensional levels? Each aspect of your mind, body, and spirit has an energetic dimension. The number and explanation of dimensional levels is argued among the scientific and spiritual worlds. But in any case, know that there are more levels of dimension than we need to be aware of at this point in our lives. We live in a 3rd dimension of the physical world where our physical senses are utilized to perceive our world. The 4th and 5th dimensions, for our purposes, will be identified as the entrance of the spirit realm; from ego to the heart.

In any case, you are here to seek what matters the most to you, what you perceive as a fulfilling life. We tend to have more of a perception problem than a lack of skills problem. Your perception has created a belief system in you that tells you what you can and cannot do. Have you ever had someone tell you that "you have so much potential locked up inside of you"? It's enough for you to want to punch them square in the face because they tend to not tell you what they see! I've been there! Some of it has been dictated to you till you perceived it as your own truth, and some of it has been a slow resistance to what is true to you; a running away from what feels right to you.

How do we exercise your perception? It's very simple... you STOP and think for a moment. Then you choose (using your ability to reason) to RESPOND in a manner that does not come from your ego; it comes from the heart (using your energetic memory in the spaces). As Epictetus, a Greek philosopher said: *"you have two ears and one mouth, use them in that proportion."*

Imagination

Our imagination is one of the most underutilized spiritual assets in today's society. It is one that gets pushed to the side while we allow the distractions of our outside world to run our minds without skipping a beat. Over time our imagination grows weak, eventually only being used to think about lack and limitation.

As a child, your mind ran wild with the clouds as it turned into animals prancing across the sky. Every box became a spaceship riding up to the moon for the day's exploration. Then suddenly, you were asked to sit still, pay attention, and stop looking out the windows. The imagination grew weary. This is the part of our spirit that shows us, in pictures, what we feel. Conditions of your past dictate your emotional association to an image. Your imagination can run wild to surround you with a beautiful scene or it can create more of the prison you believe you live in. Imagination is the asset of movie-making, it is the creative side of you that can create and move things into form just by grabbing ahold of the idea. Everything that has been created in the world has been created in the mind long before physical form. The idea was sparked from a desire or curiosity to improve; to help a community, a tribe, or your family. Imagination is a form of expansion, and expansion is what we must do.

The beautiful thing about imagination is that it can be utilized in each spiritual asset. If I said "picture a rose petal"... you will notice an experience matched with a feeling come onto the screen of your mind. This is where all of your spiritual assets are being utilized at once. Your memory recalls an event, your will then holds the image in your mind, your imagination plays out scenarios within seconds, your perception then picks apart each scenario, and then the final piece comes into play; your intuition, to tell you what is true to you. Your truth is then tested when you enter the ego in a manner that may or may not be for the growth and expansion of love, that will determine if anything created from that will or will not last.

Intuition

Intuition is defined as "the ability to understand something immediately, without the need for conscious reasoning." Essentially, it is tuning in to your gut feelings. Understanding and applying the foundational concepts of your spiritual assets will help you strengthen your inner world, thereby transforming your external reality. Intuition represents a profound knowing that doesn't require justification. It serves as an inner guide, connecting you to the infinite, to universal consciousness, to whatever you may call the source or guides. The term "intuition" itself can be dissected to "in-tuition," where "tuition" implies teaching or instructing. Thus, intuition can be viewed as receiving instruction or guidance from within.

Once you understand how your intuition manifests, you can consciously align with this internal guidance. This alignment is what many strive to achieve—to know and maintain faith in the direction it points you. Intuition doesn't pause to explain; it simply indicates the path, and you must maintain the faith to follow it. For instance, consider a time when, while driving home, you felt a sudden urge to take a different route, only to discover later that there had been an accident on your usual path, which you avoided thanks to your intuitive detour. Learn to appreciate the mysteries of your intuition. Embrace its role in your life, as it is meant to connect you with all that exists, all that has existed, and all that will exist. It is the universe nudging you towards your true center.

Explore the Tools

Let's start by exercising the spiritual assets one by one. It is important that you take a situation you have been trying to work through for a period of time. The reason for this is for you to have some time built in the direction of your unwanted patterns. This gives you an opportunity to see where your mind would normally go and when you stop listening to your heart.

Reason

Using your reasoning mind, and begin to reason yourself into a decision toward a yes answer:

____

____

____

____

____

____

____

____

____

____

____

____

____

____

____

____

____

____

____

Now take the same situation and reason yourself out of it:

____

____

____

____

____

____

____

____

____

____

____

____

____

____

____

Looking back to your answers, which one was easier to do? Then go back to the answer that was easier for you to answer and **underline** the patterns of thought that tend to trail off into a nightmare of scenarios in which you need more paper to explain it.

Next, where do you believe these ideas came from and do you have a personal experience to match that idea in your mind? Explain.

Now you can apply these questions to any decision or situation you need to reason yourself to find your logic, or patterned way of thinking.

Will

Your will is a helpful tool in using your mind to refocus and prioritize as you expand. This inward journey is going to hit some sore spots that will break free as you use your will to focus on your truth.

Using what you have identified as your values, explain below what has been stopping you from living those values. Focus on opening the heart and understand why these are so important to you. Notice where you are programmed to use a story that keeps your will focused on either a positive or negative outcome.

____
____
____
____
____
____
____
____
____
____
____
____
____
____

Now looking at the situation you identified in your reasoning exercise, how have you used your will in recreating that pattern again and again?

____
____

____

____

____

____

____

____

____

____

____

____

____

____

____

____

____

____

____

____

____

Memory

Take the same situation and try to remember when this pattern began as a child. Look for a root that has equaled out to a similar feeling as your unwanted result.

____

____

____

____

Perception

Thinking about only YOU in this situation, coming from a neutral state where you can respond from a higher vantage point. How would you perceive the situation differently now from the heart rather than the ego?

____

____

____

____

____

____

____

____

____

____

____

____

____

____

____

____

____

____

____

____

Imagination

Now for the fun part. Use your imagination to go through the situation again and rewrite using all of your spiritual assets. Take your time as this is practice using this in your everyday life.

____

____

____

Intuition

One way to help you develop your intuition is to ask yourself a question and sit with it for a moment, and the first response comes from your intuition. Anything that follows it is your mind. Practice trusting yourself when you receive an answer after you have asked a question from a neutral state.

Another way to develop your intuition is by writing a question down and allowing yourself to write. At first, you will feel like you are forcing it, but then it starts to flow. This is what we call automatic writing. This is when you can have a written dialog with your intuition, which is linked to the universal consciousness. Trust this process as you develop and attune your intuition.

Question:

____

____

____

____

Start writing until you feel your mind lets go:

____

____

____

____

____

____

____

____

____

____

____

____

____

____

____

____

____

____

____

8

The Map Begins with Thinking

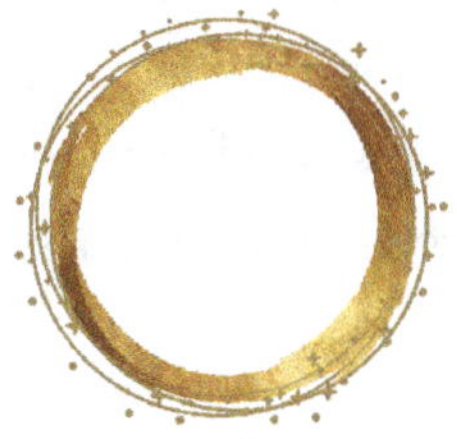

"Open your mind to the knowing that shapes your possibilities." ~ Sarah Breen

"The portal to our infinite inner worlds, cradles around us with its golden light." ~ Leslie Baker

Now that we have laid the foundation of your spiritual assets, we need to begin with an image of your map. Traditional mind mapping takes an idea and creates branches off of it to organize your thoughts. However, here we do things a bit differently. We are mapping through your mind to find the spark of your spirit and let the flame do the rest. This is your own unique roadmap for your personal journey and evolution through this lifetime. We have evolved so quickly in a short amount of time due to technology. If used correctly, technology can indeed facilitate a quantum leap within your lifetime. Here is the best part: by working on yourself, you are benefiting mass consciousness, immediate family, and past, present, and future lifetimes. How? Well, that is for you to find out – and you will rather quickly. The mysteries of this specific universe are so profound that if we started off telling you how it would benefit everyone, you would get an immediate headache as our minds are not equipped with the capacity to understand existence without time. It is your job to focus only on YOU as we move through this process. It will ripple out exactly where it needs to go to benefit all.

The roadmap begins with an image we must understand; our mind. Mind is in every cell of your physical body and beyond. It is one with all and all within one. As humans, we have free will. This free will grants us two parts of our mind, conscious and unconscious.

Conscious Mind

The conscious mind is where our ability to reason, imagine, and hold intentions resides. Our physical senses are also picked up by the conscious mind: see, hear, smell, taste, touch. Why is it that when someone loses a physical sense their energy senses are amplified? That is because our physical senses only tell us what is in the physical reality right here, right now; the illusion. When one loses their sense of sight, their unconscious sight is awakened—the ability to see through their spiritual sight. We develop our own logic in the conscious mind, and when it is in alignment with our center, we operate from that as our truth. Here is where we choose our story. Here is where we take the data from our unconscious mind and make a map between the two in coming home to our truth. Yes, it is our logical mind, but as we stated before, know what you value consciously and link it to your heart.

Unconscious Mind

The unconscious mind is where our intuition and memory reside. It's where some believe the soft nudges come from. For all intents and purposes, you can look at your unconscious mind as being connected to all that was, will be, and is. Some say it's the mass consciousness or universal mind. Your ability to use your intuition is about getting your conscious and unconscious minds to align long enough so you can create a new pattern of thought or belief.

There is great power behind our thoughts. To see the power in a thought, ask yourself these questions: Where did the idea or thought come from? Why am I entertaining this idea? Is this a good idea? So many of these questions put you in a position to work with your spiritual assets. Your thinking is 100% independent from your current reality. Take a moment to read that line again. What is happening to you right now just is. It has been created from past decisions (consciously or unconsciously made), actions to counteract reactions, and so on. You are the cause, and the now is the effect. IT JUST IS... now leave it be! Stop focusing so much on what is right in front of you and start exploring within your core. We want you, just for a brief moment, to envision a highway between your minds, core self, and your spirit. If you know that your core and spirit are only of pure love and joy, then what do you think is the issue here? The MIND! You can learn everything about the mind and still, at the end of the day, need to throw it all out! Because in the end, all you need is to know on a heart level what you value, what you love, what brings you joy, and your unconscious mind will begin to reflect more of that. You can learn and devour all the knowledge you want, but in the end, KNOW THYSELF through how you feel and operate within an open mind and heart.

At this point now, we need to take responsibility for the blocked highway we have created within ourselves. Be 100% OK with this. Be still and open. Find what works for you to help you be more open. Taking responsibility does NOT mean it's all your fault that so and so did this or that to you. We cannot control anyone else's decisions, behaviors, or reactions, only our own. Do not spend any time wondering why things happened the way they did or how it could have been different. You may or may not have seen or felt the massive detour signs or roadblocks between your mind and your core spirit. Just with your intention alone to unblock the highway, you will experience events that SHOW you an open highway. You do NOT need to DO anything at the moment. Just hold a space of intent that this shall be done and be open to what's to come. Intention is more powerful to the unconscious and spirit than physical action. JUST BE!

Thinking

Your mind has created a set of beliefs that have determined your ideas of what is right and wrong, good and bad, and so on. We need to help you release the roadblocks you have placed between your mind, heart, and spirit.

Conscious Mind: Start by taking your value statements from chapter 4 and link each one to a situation where you can change your perspective to be in alignment with that value, what your heart wants.

Value 1 Example: _______________________________

____

____

____

____

____

Value 2 Example: _______________________________________

Value 3 Example: _______________________________________

Value 4 Example: ____

Value 5 Example: ____

____

____

____

____

____

____

____

____

____

____

____

____

Unconscious Mind: To ignite the mind and heart to communicate in a manner that is for your best interest we have to get a hold of those thoughts that are governed by a pattern that doesn't serve you.

Take a thought pattern that normal plagues your mind with no answer in sight and apply it to the questions below:

Where do you believe this idea or thought pattern came from?

____

____

____

____

____

____

____

____

____

____

____

____

____

Why am I playing with this idea? Is it linked to a core value? Explain.

____

____

____

____

____

____

____

____

____

____

____

Is this idea going to help me or take me away from my heart desire?

____

____

____

____

____

____

____

____

____

____

____

____

____

Responsibility:

Am I willing to take responsibility for my thought patterns to date?
Why or why not?

____

____

____

____

____

____

____

____

____

____

____

____

____

____

Are my thoughts creating my future? If so, explain below if you
continue the same patterns what do you think it will yield you?

Understand that you have had a recurring roadblock or red flag from your heart before the thought is put into action. Identify what you think your red flag signs have been and how you plan to operate with them from now on?

9

Fear and Success

"Align to the frequency of curiosity to create space for healing to take place." ~ Sarah Breen

"Free from any weights, Mother Earth releases her wings, that are ready to fly with the flow of her heart. " ~ Leslie Baker

Fear has plagued us for generations. It is a man-made emotion, and if you enjoy history, you can trace back through time to see that each and every war was initiated from a fear of losing power.

The phrase "holding the power" seems ironic to us. Everyone holds the same amount of power, but some channel it in a healing way, while others use it to create good. Then, there are those who do not channel any power but attempt to take it from others. We may feel physically tired, but our power never diminishes. We can allow fear to create more realities that are not true to our core, or we can accept them for what they are and dismiss them without a second thought. Remember, you can only control YOU and your internal landscape and influence. If you consistently ask yourself the right questions, fear will begin to dissipate. You will focus on yourself and your relationship with your innermost truth. Fear stems from the ego, which is disconnected from your true self. The ego pushes ideas, beliefs, and conditions onto others. Are you burdened with someone else's insecurities or losses? When the ego strikes, love is far removed from it. Only by shifting your focus to love and joy can you remove fear from the thoughts in your mind. Know what you can control and understand your truth in any situation.

What's really happening in your mind and spirit is a clash of vibrations or frequencies that don't align. In your mind, you've created a fear response to an idea over which you have no control, often involving other people or entities acting independently of your desires. Your core or spirit, which only vibrates with love and joy, becomes disconnected because it does not engage with lower vibrations. This turns into a battle within the mind. Your conscious mind has created fear based on a single idea. Your subconscious mind, filled with experiences, equates only to feeling vibrations. It then recalls to the conscious mind a matching feeling vibration, and the conscious mind colors the experience based on that feeling, resulting in a relivable fear before you take your next breath. It's more like lightning striking between the conscious and subconscious minds, but you neglect your core during this process. We call this being head-focused instead of heart-focused.

How do we become heart-focused?

Let's turn fear into an experiment. Most fears revolve around the need or desire for things to be a certain way, controlling a situation unconsciously. We have become a species so prone to overthinking that we live in constant fear of an uncontrolled outcome—the unknown. Imagination is a powerful tool when used correctly. Asking "What is the worst thing that could happen?" is perhaps the worst question for an over-thinker with an active imagination. Instead, recognize that not everything needs to be perfect and accept that everything that happens is for your highest and best good, based on where you stand right now. Love where you are at this moment and give yourself permission to relax! Your fear was created to please others, not yourself. To please your core, you must stay true to it. Remaining in a state of love and joy as much as you can will help you release false fears. Wherever you focus your emotions, your outcomes will manifest accordingly. The quicker you can shift your focus, the sooner you will see better results. It takes practice. Experiment for yourself so you can free yourself from the chains of man-made emotions.

This leads us to the topic of success, the antithesis of fear. Success is uniquely defined by each individual. When I reflected on this topic after many fear responses, I engaged in an active writing dialogue to process it. Here's a journal entry to illustrate how you might dialogue with yourself about your own definition of success:

"What does success mean? It could be a perspective, a motive, or a driving point. But what is driving you? What drives your success, and who is at the wheel? Is it the need for more money, the need to get ahead, the need to fill a void, the need for approval, or something else?

*Success, in my eyes, is a decision about the outcome you want to **feel** in life. Voices may tell you, 'go to school, get a job, and you will be happy.' But what is happiness then? Happiness is a feeling of pleasure or contentment. If success was equivalent to happiness, then why do so many successful individuals live in a quiet state of sorrow?*

Why do people suddenly become inspired to live a life of pure happiness when faced with a terminal illness? Why do they find joy when their life is nearing an end? Why are the old wise, and the young not? Why do people see the beauty of life when they witness the birth of a child, only to forget that joy soon after they settle into routine?

When all that you are and all that you have may disappear tomorrow, what would your happiness be? To me, happiness is now. It is seeing the beauty in this experience we call life and all that we are presently intertwined with.

I used to carry a great sorrow within me because I lost my definition of success, my meaning of happiness. Your job, income, illness, or circumstances do not define you. You define your happiness, your success.

And when you search for it, it will be there. You need to feel your happiness one day, one moment, one experience at a time until it becomes so clear that you realize it's been there all along.

So, tell me then... What is your true happiness? Your true definition of success?"

Fear

Fear is a significant topic when it comes to facing the unknown. However, without a healthy dose of fear, the experience wouldn't be as emotionally charged with excitement upon completion. "YES, I knew I could do it!" We are here to LIVE and FEEL our lives to the fullest. Now, it's time to dive into your perceptions of fear and success.

In your honest opinion of yourself, how do you tend to utilize your own power? How and why? *(ex. Do you give it away often? Take from others by looking for someone else to make you feel better? Stand in your own power grounded? Etc)*

____

____

____

____

Holding the idea of your next desired outcome, what fear do you hold before stepping towards it? Is it a story or experienced situation that has played out over and over again? Explain.

____

____

____

____

____

____

____

____

____

____

____

____

____

____

____

____

____

____

____

____

Are these fears coming from the ego or heart? What helps you determine it? Explain.

____

____

____

____

____

If you were to experiment with the ideas that have stopped you from moving forward, what would you change in your mind in order to see if the fear has truth to it? *Hint: Is it your idea or someone else's? If you ask your heart what do you FEEL?*

____

____

____

____

____

____

____

____

____

What does success mean to you? Do an active writing session where you write the question and allow yourself to write without thinking. This is called an active writing session where you start by consciously asking yourself a question and then allow your unconscious mind to come through. This takes some practice. Take several days if not weeks practicing in a notebook to help you on this journey.

____

____

____

____

____

____

____

____

____

____

____

10

Gratitude Simplified

We all know that in every situation, we should be grateful for what we have—life, sustenance, running water, shelter, income, and/or family. However, it can be challenging to find something to be grateful for during times of despair or heartbreak. It takes time to center your-self in the situation and recognize the power of the lesson presenting itself, a reflection of your own emotional state. This is what we call fine-tuning the heart. The heart is a simple yet complex energy. It is a separate energy that vibrates differently from the rest of you. Without your heart, you would not be here. Your gratitude or appreciation must come from your heart, not your mind. While listing things to be grateful for is helpful, it doesn't always connect you to the core feeling within your heart. Your heart is tuned to your center and simplifies everything your mind overcomplicates. Your emotions could be seen as an argument between the mind and the heart. You "know" what needs to be done, but your mind—occupied with thoughts about priorities, situations, other people, work, etc.—gets in the way. We then find ourselves off-center once again, caught in a windstorm of confusion and thoughts of scarcity.

How do you simplify the heart process?

By asking yourself what your heart desires most. Quickly write down the five most important things to you and then assess whether each one truly aligns with your heart's desires (exercise below). I find that most people don't mention specifics, but rather general feelings that they can describe. That's when you know you are getting closer to your heart's desires. Your heart will never evoke a negative emotion about a thought. If you experience a negative emotion, you have strayed from your heart's desire. If you feel calm, relief, contentment, and bliss, then you're beginning to connect with your heart's desire, your simplified way of expressing gratitude.

Life is simple, and your heart bears witness to the simplicity of nature and its cycles. Every person has their own cycle that creates the rhythm of the physical world around them. The ebb and flow of every moment are like a heartbeat, inhalation, and exhalation. Trees dance in the wind, rain taps out its own song, and ocean waves breathe in and out as the sand dances with them. Everything in life is in a state of balance. When a hole or footprint is created in the sand, water fills the space faster than you can dig or walk. When you can quiet your thoughts of negative emotions, ideas, and situations, you begin to use your intentional focus—or your will—to feel your heart's desire in every moment. Your heart fills the spaces just as water and sand at the beach. Use your will to focus on what matters most to your heart. Your heart exists only in the moment.

Your heart knows the way, and you must learn to follow it. This is another way of describing following your intuition.

By following your heart, you can move from a state of lack to manifesting in physical form. This process takes time, depending on how deep you've gone into the rabbit hole of lack and scarcity. But don't berate yourself for where you are or try to justify why you are there. That only distances you further from your heart. This is where getting to know your spiritual assets can help you adopt enlightened thought processes, debunk thoughts that weren't yours to begin with, and verbalize your emotions to reconnect with your heart's desire. This creates your new proprietary logic based solely on your core and heart center.

Thinking is a great tool to start with, as we need to know where we are without pointing fingers or justifying why. Then we move into the heart, feeling your emotions and asking if this aligns with what your heart truly wants. You can phrase it any way that feels right to you, but essentially, you're asking, "How does my core feel about this?" Start with something easy that you love dearly (children, animals, nature, hiking, etc.) and feel into the moment with it until you can describe it in words for yourself. Create a picture in your mind (imagination) and focus on it (will) until it feels completely normal to feel that way every day. This will help you detect when you're off your heart center and dancing in the mind again. This process should not be forced; nothing from the heart or your spirit is forced. It's a gentle process that will teach you how to be easy with yourself. If something requires force, it will feel like you're swimming against the current. Your response should be to create space and flow with your heart. It's about finding your own balance within yourself, a rhythm that is unique to you and flows easily from the heart. Your manifestations will match your connection to the heart. This means your immediate manifestations will be how the next person interacts with you or the next thing you stumble across. The red road in Native American culture is about following the spiritual life guided by your heart, using compassion as your compass. It will never steer you wrong. Trusting your process on this journey allows you to empower yourself and grow to a new level each day.

Gratitude Explained

Gratitude is a spiritual skill that needs to be expressed both energetically, in the fourth dimension, and physically, in the third dimension. It is the language of the heart. Someone may verbalize that they are grateful, but you can often feel if their energy tells a different story. This is evident when you ask someone how they are doing, and they reply with "everything is wonderful," yet their face and energy clearly communicate the opposite. We must stop lying to ourselves. You should be aware that it hurts your soul every time you lie to it, and your heart.

Gratitude needs to be simplified for your soul to begin feeling trusted. Your priorities may have been skewed by societal ideas of what life should or shouldn't be. Stop focusing on what's out there and start focusing on what's within YOU.

What are the 5 MOST IMPORTANT things to you?

1.____

____

____

____

2.

3.

4.

5.

Now ask yourself, in what way does this make your heart sing? Answer for each of the 5 that you listed above. *Note: Your heart will never give you a negative emotion surrounding the idea. The emotions are your indicator if you are coming from a place of heart centered gratitude or the mind, ego, etc.*

1.

2.

3.

4.

5.

Make gratitude a practice, just like meditation, journeying, yoga, and other human skills we use to tap into the spiritual realm, the 4th dimension. These skills are crucial for the upliftment of our species and planet. They allow everyone to create a well-tuned vessel for the soul, enabling your heart to live to its fullest as intended upon your arrival here. Since everything is composed of geometric shapes that resonate at specific frequencies, it's essential to align yourself with higher frequencies. However, you can't transition from a very low frequency to a higher one without experiencing some pain.

Pain! You may think, "I didn't sign up for this!" But let me explain. Pain, whether felt physically or emotionally, places you in a pressure tank that facilitates a jump in vibration. How you feel directly correlates with where you are in the frequency range. There are infinite frequencies in the universe, so you don't need to aim for the top; instead, simply aspire to evolve to the next frequency. Pain is present to help you recognize where you are, where you've been, and where you want to go. PERIOD. So, use gratitude to propel you to where you want to be! It's that simple. I had a loving and sarcastically humorous grandmother I called Vava growing up. Her laugh could turn your frown upside down within milliseconds. I use her image, her voice, her laugh, and her gentle yet sarcastic tone to snap me out of lower frequencies and into gratitude, my heart center, because to me, she was always heart-centered.

So, choose an image, experience, sensation, or something that can anchor you to a feeling of gratitude before you start spiraling down the rabbit hole of misery. I used my late grandmother as my example. Search your mind until you can feel your mind sync with your heart. Find an anchor point that you can use quickly before being taken down the rabbit hole. Describe it below. Print it out and keep it handy. This is a skill! Use this skill to help yourself ascend the frequency ladder to your desires.

____

____

____

11

Balance

"Creating life with a heart centered intention creates the song of your life." ~ Sarah Breen

"With eyes aligned to our souls' flow, the whale glides through the waters of life." ~ Leslie Baker

Everyone seeks balance, even if they cannot verbalize it initially. Work life, family life, social life, vacation life—these are all viewed as separate spheres of your life that need to be balanced. This separation often leads to the frantic life of someone who believes they have absolutely no time to do anything, ultimately giving up and allowing one segment of their life to dominate everything else, drowning in the rat race we call "the struggle." Consequently, balance then begins to feel like a task in itself. New parents struggle to find some kind of balance in the ever-changing routine of an infant; a student struggles to find balance with school after returning from summer vacation; and a retiree struggles to find balance in their newfound freedom from the forty-year rat race. The word "struggle" is so often placed in front of the act of finding balance that it has truly become a manifestation of a struggle to achieve it. But what if you change the dialogue within the words? It begins to change the feeling that comes out of the statement. For example: First-time parents found balance as their infant progressed in a healthy routine, the student found balance quickly due to excitement coming back from summer vacation, and the new retiree found fun balance quickly as he filled his time with activities he always enjoyed. Changing the dialogue within the context of the idea makes a world of difference in terms of your feelings because it paints a different picture. It is a pleasant expectation and not one that is seen as a struggle from the perspective of mass consciousness.

We already know that all words carry significant meaning, which you then internalize. This is where we would benefit the most from learning to create with intention. Understanding your own inner dialogue about ideas and situations is a key component to creating and living with intention. Every situation is about perspective, not description. When you feel that a situation has happened to you, you will always approach things from the stance of victimhood and never from the heart. Manifestation in physical form is always formed from your feelings about any topic. If you choose to feel from the victim state, then that is what you will feel over and over again until you take a hard look at your inner dialogue. When you change the words attached to a situation, you create new linked emotions, high vibrations, and a more relatable picture in your mind. Step-by-step, the outer situation will begin to mimic the inner dialogue as long as you believe that is so. We will tap into this in a later chapter, but for now, start with becoming aware of the feelings you hold behind the inner dialogue inside.

Knowing where you are is a large part of it. Even though time is moving and every moment quickly transitions into the past, your understanding of your state of being (vibration) will help you identify where you are and where you would like to be next. I say "NEXT" because you will never reach your final destination—the destination will always change because life in the physical dimension is about the process. Each goal we reach leads to another, and another, and so on. Some people believe that your career or education marks the beginning of your final destination, while others believe retirement is the destination. If your focus is too far off into a future that is forever changing and moving, then your manifestations in the physical will remain in the future state. What you "DO" for work or what your goals are is NOT who you are or where you are going. What you do in life can only be identified as a result of how you feel every day. Granted, you will have days or moments when you feel off, but the majority of the time you should be centered on feelings that you identify as good. Intention moves quicker into manifestation if you lead with how you feel most of the time while changing that inner dialogue to what feels better. Your TRUE IDENTITY is not your job title, degree, relationships, or social status; it is how you feel each day and how you maneuver those feelings while interacting with other people. Your true identity is your... BALANCE!

Balance is something that can easily manifest if you center back to everything we have been discussing so far; be easy with yourself, give yourself permission to find your true nature, acknowledge and move forward with your feelings, and change the dialogue in your mind to what feels better. Once you begin to feel good more often, your mind starts to compartmentalize what is important to you, what makes sense, what you should start to question, and what your own unique truth about your life is. Your balance will begin when you pay less attention to other opinions, conversations, and actions and are truly comfortable with yourself. You should understand by now that this is their journey, not yours to interject into. Balance is knowing when to let go of your idea of control over others and focus on what you can control—only YOU. If your mind goes "but, but, but..." remember that it is your mind and ego talking, not your spirit. Your spirit immediately says "FINALLY," while your conditioned mind has excuses to not relinquish its tight grip on a false reality.

At first, you may hate this idea. You may laugh at it. You may roll your eyes and play with all the recurring feelings until you hit a wall again. Either way, there will be a part of you that desires to feel centered and balanced; and through that one desire, you will begin to see your walls coming down. Start to detach yourself from what some material things or relationships make you feel and focus on what is important to the center of you. Focus on fun, joy, bliss, happiness, and most of all... love.

Seeking Balance

Balance is another skill we must teach ourselves to continue evolving. Your body, mind, emotions, and heart will indicate whether or not you are balanced at any given moment. Because we are so focused on language, we must start by examining our inner dialogue to figure out where the hang-ups are. Again, this involves being truthful with yourself and not deceiving your heart. Consider the person in the front row who claims, "I am happy!" yet their face looks stone-cold. A truly happy "look" is an energy that lights up a room with their presence. The inner dialogue is the key to illuminating what's inside.

Take a common theme in your mind that tends to leave you feeling in the dumps. Write out the common dialog or bullet point it down below.

____

____

____

____

____

____

____

____

____

____

____

____

____

____

____

____

Now take this dialog above and re-read it. Write below how it should really sound by changing the words or taking negative words out. This takes a good amount of brain power so do not get frustrated. It's like riding a bike without training wheels, takes time to gain the right balance.

____

____

____

____

____

____

____

____

____

____

____

____

____

____

After reading the chapter, what can you identify as your true identity? What do you desire to FEEL each day, how you interact, how to dance with your existence here and now? This is a deep question so take your time with it. Allow yourself to feel, cry, scream, etc. Your heart needs to be expressed.

____

____

____

____

____

____

____

____

____

____

12

Belief and Faith

"Faith is knowing the caterpillar never knew it was a butterfly until it flew." ~ Sarah Breen

"Allowing its cocoon to cradle the journey of its transformation, the butterfly now shines its full golden radiance." ~ Leslie Baker

Belief and faith have different meanings. For our purposes, we will define belief as a conditioned pattern of thought that has created your own logic, while faith involves learning to trust without needing an explanation for why or how. Each person has their own beliefs and places their faith in whatever they acknowledge as a higher power or centered energy force. Belief can usually be bolstered with evidence and facts until you accept it as a truth for yourself. Each organized religion has a doctrine of faith, and each person has their own beliefs that determine their level of faith. It is your own experience that determines if something moves from a belief to faith.

Now let's turn your attention back to you and your own beliefs. Believing in yourself is the first step in consciously creating your manifesting world. "Believe in yourself" may seem like a platitude when someone doesn't understand how terrifying it can be to take action. But we are going to take a much closer look at YOU than you ever thought possible. Depending on where you currently are, you have a set of beliefs that influence how you view the world, how your inner dialogue operates, and how you feel from day to day. It is experience-based, meaning what you have experienced to date conditions what you believe is right and wrong, good and bad. As you seek balance in your world, your world will reflect back what you believe to be true. Call it the law of attraction or whatever you wish, but the truth is that your beliefs can keep you in a holding pattern for as long as you allow them to influence your mind. Believing in yourself—your perception of your ability to be or have anything in this lifetime—is your first step toward having faith in yourself.

Faith is your ability to have confidence in your role within the creation process of manifestation. You are responsible for remembering your center—the center you gradually forgot as you woke up in this human life. Children understand much more than we as adults could ever comprehend about the "truth" of life. Allow them to be themselves and watch as they bloom into the spirits they desired to be before they were born. Your faith is more than what you deem as your higher power; it is your moment-to-moment feeling of complete joy and love for everything you encounter in this lifetime, trusting your journey. Keep in mind that a person who has strong "faith" knows that where there is darkness, light can flood the room faster than flipping a light switch. It's about completely letting go and relaxing into the unknown without expectation of a specific path; it's about releasing the how and allowing your feeling of the outcome to manifest for the good. Your beliefs—your experience-based ideas—will keep your faith from growing if you do not allow yourself to acknowledge your feelings from moment to moment. Your feelings will help you discern whether you are experiencing faith (spirit-guided) or belief (conditioned ideas and experiences). Again, your inner dialogue will play a key role in helping you determine if something has moved from a belief to complete faith.

When you start to move from having ideas about a topic to having faith, the emotions surrounding it become clearer. We are born to create the world around us, and with a growing faith within yourself, you will see the manifestations in physical form. Time will feel like it slows down and speeds up when you desire it to. You naturally let go of the how and allow the universe to fill in the details of how while you savor the experience. When something "bad" happens, remember that it is a perceived belief transitioning to a balanced state, like how a pendulum swings. It shows you what is out of balance. Balance is then experienced, and you begin to let go of what no longer serves you in this ever-growing state. Please understand that if you have a very strong desire stemming from emotions other than love and joy, then time needs to elapse for your belief to transform into faith for the desired outcome. You may be putting too many specifics on the path, and the beliefs or emotions behind it are keeping you in a holding pattern. This is common in our overthinking world now, which is why some people decide that the law of attraction does not work. Do not waste any time trying to dissect how you came to these limiting beliefs; instead, allow your feelings to move from ideas of lack to expansion and bliss. You will know you have started to shift when inspiration strikes that feels exciting and uplifting.

Faith is Needed

Belief and faith need to be addressed. We must identify what you believe to be true versus trusting the unknown. This is a big jump for many, but you will not be thrust into the dark unwillingly. The beautiful thing about this great mystery, which has many names—the divine, the source, the universe, God, or whatever you call your higher power—is that you will take incremental steps toward your own unique unfolding into the unknown. So, don't be scared of the words. Know that we once understood what was in the unknown and chose to come into this human existence to forget on purpose. Why, you may ask? Because that is the process of having a physical experience. LIFE is a gift.

After reading the chapter, what is your perceived belief of your ability to be and have the desires you have stated? Take into consideration the language you use as it indicates the exercise from the previous chapter.

____

____

____

____

____

____

____

____

____

____

____

____

____

____

____

Shift your perspective to a childlike state. Find a situation you feel is the unknown or scary and come from the perspective of a child. They always see the brighter side of the situation or instead they redesign it to match them in the moment to moment of the story. Practice below. Take a journal and do this activity often to help you through situations to move from belief to faith.

____

____

____

____

____

____

____

____

____

____

____

____

____

____

____

Knowing where a desire is on the Belief – Time – Faith scale:

It is important to get to know your own patterns of thought that can easily be switched from belief to faith, and then there are others that need time to manifest.

Take 5 desires, the things most important to you, and ask yourself if it is a belief (conditioned ideas) or faith (childlike excitement, a knowing). If you're not sure the place TIME next it to as you need some experience to help you find out if it is belief or faith.

1.____

____

____

____

____

2.____

____

____

____

____

3.____

____

____

____

____

4.____

____

____

____

____

5.____

____

____

____

13

Determining Goals or Focus Points

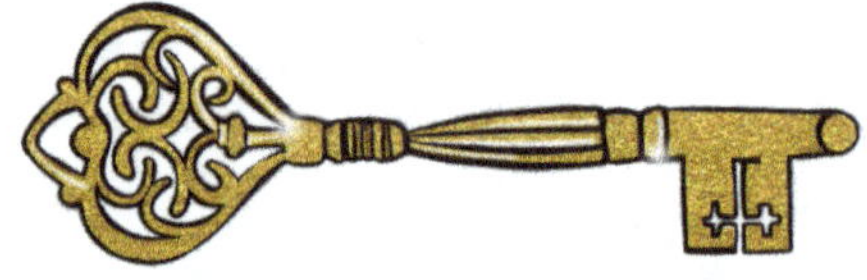

"Choice is the key you hold close to your heart." ~ Sarah Breen

"When we are ready to walk through the door, we will find the key within us that fits the lock." ~ Leslie Baker

Now, onto the old topic of goals. This is an outdated way of doing things. As I became a "thinker" and paralyzed myself with lists of goals and desires, I felt like I was on a sinking ship with no rescue boat in sight. That being said, I am not a fan of overthinking goals and making long lists of wants if you're completely stuck in a holding pattern. Some people can take one goal and cling to it like a dog on a bone. Others, like myself, choose to explore life, spirit, and the inner workings of the universe over a goal for a new car. I was never happy reporting my biggest goal to my mentors because it made me feel like I could never achieve it. I would cry out in desperation as my results kept getting worse instead of better. That was when I knew goal setting was not my cup of tea.

In my early 20s, my life began to fall apart. I turned to drugs and alcohol, hoping they would fill the deep void inside me. The day I tried to take my life, my one-year-old rescue dog sat at my feet, begging me to smile, to laugh, and to stop what I was doing. I looked into the eyes of the one I had chosen to be my pal for life and made another choice: "I will try for you." I share this to underline the importance of CHOICE! Goals need a new understanding—they are a choice, a leaping-off point, a no-turning-back decision, something you feel deep within even if you haven't felt much up to that point. People have experiences like this all the time. Mine was linked with my dog because animals have always been my safe place; the best way Spirit could reach me. As a child, I could sit in the grass all day with my dog and feel completely free and loved.

It's the feelings that help you see through the mind and into the heart.

Goals are focus points, not destinations. They are like the star stickers you receive as a child for potty training or getting a good grade on your report card. Goals have unique meanings based on your beliefs. If you come from a competitive upbringing, you may thrive off of goals and tasks, while others who were condemned for not reaching a goal may harbor negative beliefs about them. Focus points are based on feelings, then articulated into "goals." If you continue to ignore your feelings, then the same cycles will persist until you make a new choice to address them. Your focus points should be feelings that matter the most to you: love, comfort, freedom, and joy. Then allow the universe or your higher power to guide your journey. You are solely responsible for yourself and your own inner dialogue. Asking yourself and the invisible forces around you (even if you don't understand what they are) for help will allow the universe to assist you along the way. We made a choice to be here, to wake up, to keep moving forward. We make the choice to relive a cycle or break it. You can demand in your mind to break a cycle, but if you are not aligned with your heart on that topic, it will continue to repeat.

You will need to identify if an idea or focus point you are reaching for is truly your own or someone else's. We are distracted by social media and conversations that implant ideas of what happiness or success looks like according to the masses. If you are unsure whether your focus point is genuinely your idea, simply ask that question internally. Relax, and then let it go. Sit back and watch as the universe responds. Start to notice how the world answers your question through conversations, chance meetings, a phone call, or something that catches your eye. Begin to trust in the letting-go process and become more aware of the present. You may not be fully ready to heal from everything at once; remember, it's a journey. Time will begin to slow down, and your true self will start to emerge. Your focus points should be aimed at achieving a feeling that is better than your current state—a feeling you want to achieve every day. The results will manifest in your everyday life. In the beginning, all I could focus on was feeling happy in each possible moment. If I didn't focus on that, my surroundings reflected my inner frustration and anguish. I would argue with my spouse or become upset over the smallest task going awry. Once you identify your focus point and reach for it as often as you can, you will see the manifestations around you change as you transform that belief into faith.

It's never really been about goals, has it? Younger generations intuitively sense that happiness isn't obtained by driving the fastest car or owning the biggest house. They feel and know it; we just forgot. Life becomes a beautiful dance between the physical world, your mind, and your spirit. Yes, money can be a focus point, but ensure the feeling comes from a focus point that feels good and doesn't carry a laundry list of negative stories or attachments. Start small with feelings of freedom or happiness and let the world dance with you as you gain clarity on what really matters. You should now see the patterns. This has never been rocket science, yet there are thousands of marketing strategies out there claiming to show you how to become a millionaire or success magnet, when the average toddler can tell you what's most important in life. We just FORGOT! Know that all you ever NEED is your own willingness to examine your inner dialogue, feelings, and future worries in order to bring yourself back into balance with life. Be humble, be the empty cup willing to be filled with what feels true, be curious about every moment, and STOP TAKING THINGS PERSONALLY. Everyone you know and love is going through the same process in their own unique way. Be still and hold a space for yourself and loved ones to expand into what is uniquely yours to create in this reality.

Focus Points

Goals are now Focus Points for our purposes. These are your points of NEXT interest that has and underlining feeling of happiness, joy, freedom, etc. A feeling that feels better than you feel right now. Let's begin by breaking this down into reusable steps each time you make a choice for your next focus point.

List out what you really want out of life:

____

____

____

____

____

____

____

____

____

____

____

____

____

____

____

____

____

____

____

____

____

____

____

____

Now match those desires with the underlining feeling you are trying to achieve from receiving this desire:

____

____

____

____

____

____

____

____

____

____

____

Next, match those underlining feelings to the 5 most important things to you. Are they similar? Is there one key feeling you are trying to achieve? Explain.

____

____

____

____

____

____

____

____

____

____

____

____

____

What overall feeling (1) do you desire NEXT? Match the feeling to ideas you have in your mind that would help you with achieving that feeling. It does not matter how crazy it sounds, what you will need to do, or if you don't know how to do it; just write it down.

____

____

____

____

____

____

____

____

____

____

____

____

____

Now, based on what you have picked apart in your feelings field; what can you say is your next logical step towards the main feeling you desire? Explain.

____

____

____

____

____

____

____

____

____

____

____

____

____

Notice that the inner dialogue is trying to take over as you sort through your feelings. This happens because we often sweep our feelings under the rug in an attempt to maintain harmony in our surroundings. However, it may not have occurred to you that by operating from your center, harmony can be achieved without the need to force external situations. Happiness has always been an inside job, and your surroundings will reflect this at every step. Therefore, recognize that each day when you wake up, it's a new opportunity to choose your focus point. Keep reminding yourself of this and watch how your surroundings mirror your internal state.

You may need to revisit this concept often. Some days may go really well, while others may not. Understanding your focus points, dancing with your manifestations, and not taking anything personally are new perspectives that some of us may need to metaphorically tattoo on our foreheads. You are transforming beliefs into your own faith. Learn to let things go because the more emotionally charged something is in a negative way, the more challenging the manifestation will be on the other end.

14

Holding Space For What's To Come

"The sunflower holds the greatest potential in thousands of seeds as it continually reaches for the sun." ~ Sarah Breen

"Basking in the warm glow of the sun's rays of knowledge, the sunflower turns its head to the light, and hope of what's to come." ~ Leslie Baker

Holding space for the universe to fill in the gaps of what's to come will test your faith on a different level. Trusting that everything will work out for your highest good is a skill that fosters humility and calm. Staying relaxed helps you remain neutral in the present, regardless of whether things are good or bad. Staying present as much as possible allows you to release your tight grip on future predictions, which may or may not align with your heart's desires. Humility is the gracious understanding that "you don't know what you don't know." All you need to do is ask for what your heart desires and then let it go, holding infinite space for it to manifest in your physical reality. If you keep asking repeatedly, you are not truly holding space or being present. Instead, you are pushing the outcome further into the future, when the answer might already be here, right now. The immediate feelings you experience provide feedback about your connection to truth (which feels good) or to ego (a fear-based reality). This is why many gurus teach meditation as a foundational skill before imparting spiritual knowledge. One must learn to quiet the mind, feel the heart, sense the pulse of the world, notice the spaces within spaces, and achieve neutrality. Consider how frustrating it is when someone tells you to calm down while you're in a fight-or-flight state—it simply won't happen. Gurus have designed processes that demonstrate how you operate best after quieting your mind, feeling the energy that flows all around us, and becoming that energy. When you practice quieting your mind, you begin to dream, imagine, and breathe easier. What once made you frantic seems less important. In essence, you are learning to hold space for what is yet to come.

Visualizing what you desire is an effective tool in the asking process. It creates a mental bookmark to recall the feelings or vibrations that an image in your mind represents. The language of the universe isn't made up of dialects; rather, it's all about vibrations and how you interpret them. Use your feelings as a compass, moving from one focal point to another. That's why life is fun! Use your perception to view this physical life as a journey, a playground, and experiment each day on how to make the next day even better! The masses suffer from a perception problem where everyone else's perception dictates your own. If ideas don't feel good, stop giving them your attention. PERIOD! An emotional empath once told me, "You seem to be emotionless at times." I burst out laughing and responded, "I don't engage in conversations or situations that don't feel good, or where someone cannot see beyond the problem." You don't need to engage in acts that don't serve the best interest of all parties involved. It's a vicious cycle of vibrations being interpreted in a negative light rather than for what they truly are. So, do not engage. You can listen and be a helping hand in finding solutions but avoid getting involved in the vibrational drama of egos. If it doesn't feel good, then you are not holding space for things to manifest as intended. Instead, you're adding a mixture of vibrations that do not serve your highest intentions. Using such situations as feedback for your own vibrational state is also very helpful in learning how to detach from others' reactions. Cherish this feedback, even if it feels judgmental, because every moment is a teachable one towards your growth.

Epictetus stated, "You have two ears and one mouth so that we can listen twice as much as we speak." The more you speak on topics, the less you are listening from within. The more you speak, the less you can interpret vibrationally in your mind. Learning when to talk and when to listen is a valuable skill. When was the last time you heard the trees sing as the wind danced through their leaves? When was the last time you heard the rain's rhythmic beat as it danced off your roof? The more you speak, the more you justify your lack of results. Be still. Be neutral. It isn't wrong to speak, but learning when to listen will assist you in meditation, being present, and holding space for what's to come. It fosters a new level of appreciation for the physical realm we inhabit. Our world is thriving, regardless of what the media says. Appreciation means choosing to see the love, joy, and beauty all around. It doesn't require becoming a tree hugger today. Just start by appreciating where you are right here, right now. This appreciation will prevent your mind from taking over and creating a laundry list of things to do and worry about.

What can you control? Only YOU, right here, right now! Understand there's no rush to get anywhere and remain open to what's coming.

Holding a Space for YOU

Holding space for what is coming is a distinctly human skill. This can be likened to asking a toddler to have patience while you balance ten things in your arms and are unable to give them a drink immediately. You might chuckle at this analogy, but it's crucial to view yourself from the universe's perspective. Indeed, we humans can be like that impatient toddler who doesn't understand why we can't have everything right now. Why is this? Because we exist within a time-space reality that requires us to move from one point to another, aiding the process of manifestation. This is the moment when life meets us in the unfolding of manifestation at the perfect time. How you FEEL and how you concentrate on your focal point will aid you in loosening your grip on your desires. Consider the following questions to delve deeper into your desires.

Based upon your desires list at the pervious chapter, what are the ones that have some negative experiences (lack, scarcity, fear) attached to them? Which ones tend to put your mind into future worry long before the evidence appears it is true? List them out, allow your feelings to pour out. The pain needs to come to the surface in order to create space for what's to come.

____

____

____

____

____

____

____

____

____

____

____

____

____

____

Next, take a moment to take a deep breath. As you breathe in, take in all that you desire from the top of your head; as you breathe out, imagine all of that pain filters out your feet and bursts into white light. The more you visualize and breathe you will feel the shift from the core of you. Explain how you felt before and after the breathing exercise.

____

____

____

____

____

____

____

____

____

____

____

____
____
____
____
____
____
____
____
____
____
____
____
____
____
____
____
____
____

Now that you are in a neutral state, we can practice holding a space for your desired feeling. What do you feel is the truth about what you worry about? Does it hold a reoccurring pattern?

____
____
____
____
____
____
____
____

____

____

____

____

State out loud "I am an empty glass, universe what do I need to do or be today to achieve my core truth?" then write down what comes to you first.

____

____

____

____

____

____

____

____

____

____

____

____

____

____

____

Take a moment to reread what you wrote. The answers you seek are always available to you. These are skills that you can fine tune and utilize in you day to day life. Choose to listen to your inner core. When you listen, it never places you in a state of worry or fear. It will always point you in the direction of what to do or feel right now. If you begin to follow that, releasing your grip on expectations of how everything should be, then you will experience holding a space for what's to come.

15

The Art of Detachment

"Renewal is the in emptying of the mind and reaching into your roots." ~ Sarah Breen

"As the petals fall from the Cherry Blossom, she releases them, knowing their beauty is meant only for the divine time that they shine." ~ Leslie Baker

Detaching from certain thoughts, behaviors, actions, and the illusion of control is a skill seldom taught in school. Babies intuitively know their limits and needs, recognizing what they can and cannot control. This innate wisdom often becomes muddled when they learn to manipulate their abilities to please others, blurring their pure sense of self.

We've established that the only true control you possess is over yourself—your thoughts, behaviors, responses, and words. This realization implies that all experiences in your life are a result of what you've chosen to attach yourself to. Attachment to ideas and thoughts can cloud your mind and judgment. The art of detachment involves recognizing WHAT you can control within the creation process. If you only control yourself, you should keep your thoughts private until you're ready to release them. History has shown us that attachment often leads to conflict over power, territory, and people, fueled by a misguided belief in control and the resulting fear.

So, how do you learn to detach from things beyond your control? The concept is startlingly simple: acknowledge that everything is impermanent. Everything in our lives is constantly shifting and belongs to no one but the energy source from which it originated. Consider your house—it's not truly yours, nor does it belong to the bank. Reactions to a house fire can vary: some may grieve the loss of possessions, while others feel gratitude that their family survived. Ultimately, it's not about the "stuff." What matters most are the energy and love from your family, connections with community and friends. Understanding that the land you own on paper is just part of a larger, impermanent energy cycle can be liberating.

Physical possessions—houses, cars, travel experiences—enhance the physical life we are here to live. They bring joy, experiences, and fun, but they are just "stuff." Detaching from the notion of ownership shifts your focus to the essence of joy and connection these items can bring.

Our attachment to material life and survival concerns can foster deep-seated fears, driving greed, scarcity, and envy. But when you view life through the lens of potential loss, you'll begin to see the underlying beauty and love. The desire for a nice house or car is often tied to a core emotional need. Identifying this need helps you realize that while these items can enhance your experience, they are not necessary for it. There's a significant difference in perspective here.

Be open and patient with yourself. We lead subjective lives, endowed with free will. It's about living in the present, with an open heart. Every new experience is an opportunity to shed the ego's attachments and align with your inner essence. And remember, life shouldn't always be serious! Humor is essential; it breaks down barriers and lightens the burden of ego-driven desires. If it isn't about love, it's likely your ego speaking. If you worry about others' perceptions of your new path, you're prioritizing their opinions over your own valuable insights. Remember, everything is transient! Regularly check where your focus lies. If you feel anything but peace, you're likely attached to an idea, person, or situation that no longer serves you. Your ego resists change, keeping you trapped in a cycle of redundant thoughts—the inner hamster wheel. Reflect on where your energy is directed daily. Feeling connected and present in your body is crucial; too often, distractions lead us away from this state. Change and movement originate from an energy within you waiting to be awakened. Avoid letting your ego dominate, pulling you into cycles of comparison, jealousy, or anxiety through endless scrolling on social media. Stay open and patient. Observe your actions, recognize areas needing detachment, and continuously work on them.

Worry equals a negative wish!

Often, the issues that cause you the most worry are either beyond your control or simply require more time to resolve. Remember, you are not here to FIX anyone—no one is broken, no one needs fixing. Most people merely need help discovering their center and connecting with what resonates uniquely with them. Shift your focus more towards where you are investing your energy and less on fretting over uncontrollable outcomes. Engage in activities that bring you joy. Situations and their outcomes won't change unless you detach from the expected results, whether they occur or not. Your purpose is to reconnect with YOURSELF, not to complete anything or anyone else. The only real struggle is the one you impose upon yourself. There is no mission, only a journey to rediscover your core self and the abundance that can blossom from it.

A successful relationship, in any form, occurs when two complete individuals come together, each whole on their own, creating an even greater whole. It's not about your half and my half; it's about two complete wholes uniting to form something larger. Avoid excuses and unnecessary worries. Just strive to find and fully be yourself. Your journey began long before you were conceived, and every experience up to now has prepared you for the clarity you've been seeking—perhaps even desperately calling out for. Now, make space for it through the art of detachment.

I like to approach life as if beta testing everything. I treat each experience as an experiment. This mindset alleviates pressure and allows me to progress without clinging to inauthentic ideas or succumbing to the influence of others. Since everything is impermanent, why stress overly about our earthly concerns when we are here to embrace the love and support that constantly surrounds us? Take a moment to answer that for yourself.

Detaching

Understanding what you value, what is most important to you in ALL feeling states will help you with the process of detachment. Because in order for you to grow and achieve the life that has always been here for you, we must drop our beliefs surrounding the physical world.

What ideas or topics tend to place your mind in judgment, fear of losing something, or the need to control an outcome? Focus on you and where your mind tends to recall the ego and not your heart center.

____

____

____

____

____

____

____

____

____

____

____

____

Looking at your values, the 5 most important things to you, and your free will; what ideas are you willing to feed to the fire and let them go? If everything is impermanent than this is a loaded question and you will most likely ask yourself this frequently. Explain.

____

____

____

____

____

____

____

How do I know if something is coming from the ego and what is coming from my heart center?

____

____

____

____

To know when your ego is keeping you from moving forward you must list out what you use as your distractions:

____

____

____

____

____

____

____

____

____

____

____

Next, list out as many feel good activities that you can use to replace the distracted ego activities. Go simple (ex. Go for a walk, mediate, listen to music, play an instrument, etc)

____

____

____

Knowing what you know now, identify what desires you have placed a specific outcome for the result to manifest. This is similar to looking through a keyhole rather than opening the door and stepping in willingly.

Since everything is impermanent, why should we worry so much when we came here to fully embrace the love and support that is always here for you?

____

____

____

____

____

____

____

____

____

____

16

Remembering and Awakening

"Answering the call from the depth of your soul is awaken the burn of the sacred heart." ~ Sarah Breen

"Igniting the beat of our hearts, the flames of pure love flicker. "
~ Leslie Baker

As you begin to consciously forge connections with your core, take notice when the ego emerges. Living from the heart, you contribute not only to your own growth but also aid those you cherish and enhance the collective consciousness. This positively influences generational lines—past, present, and future. Remembering and awakening your core involves mastering the art of self-love. By loving yourself unconditionally, you infuse love across all dimensions of time, space, and reality. Thus, recalling your essence is a profound honor with far-reaching benefits, extending well beyond the self. Such recognition should ease any concerns about selfishness. Remember, you are never solitary in this endeavor; our ultimate purpose is to reclaim the unconditional love we've always known was ours. Be gentle with yourself. Cherish your core, your heart's deepest desires, and every breath you draw. There's no need to dictate others' needs or desires—focus solely on nurturing your connection to your core. This healing journey is uniquely yours. Embracing self-love not only honors your essence but also facilitates a healing process tailored specifically to you. Your heart might need mending before you can voice your truth, or it might be the reverse. Everyone's journey to their truth, to who they are meant to be, is distinctly personal.

Find your still point in the silence.

Resist the urge to become overwhelmed and revert to the frantic pace of life, which only serves to reinforce the ego's dominance. Once your intentions are released to the universe, the unfolding process is unstoppable. This journey is rich with variety—you might take detours, venture off the beaten path, or cruise along the main roads. Regardless of the route, the most enduring memories often come from the journey itself. Awakening involves a process of mindful thinking, making decisions that align with your greatest good, and then learning to release that thought, allowing the universe to bridge the gaps while you inhabit the present moment. Next, shift your focus to the spaces between —the inherent love in all you perceive and experience. What are these spaces between? They are the tranquility you encounter when you still your mind enough to feel your environment without needing to see it. You become attuned to the energy circulating around you until the distinction between your head and feet blurs. In these moments, unconditional love pulses through the void. This is when you rediscover what it means to simply BE, without the need for thought.

Ego or Heart?

Understanding when your ego steps in and when you are moving from your heart center is a tool you will need on this journey. It makes the journey easier for you to digest when experiences happen that may or may not have been wanted. Unconditional love is available to you every step of the way, you just need to learn when to call on it and where to find it.

From what you have learned so far, what is your interpretation of finding your way to your heart center?

____

____

____

____

____

____

____

____

____

____

____

____

____

____

Do you have any emotions push back when reading this statement: "Remembering and awakening your core is learning how to love yourself unconditionally." If so, explain what you are experiencing.

____

____

____

____

____

____

____

____

____

____

____

____

____

____

Self-love can be exercised by self-care activities. List below things you can do often enough to express love to yourself. Circle the activities that you can easily do on a regular basis. Be creative! What do you love to do or NEED to do for yourself?

____

____

____

____

____

____

____

Commit to some of the activities you listed above. By not practicing self-love you are slowly slipping your soul into sadness. When you neglect the unconditional love that is pulsing everywhere, you are creating more resistance to the process of your journey. It will then take longer, the lessons will be harder, and the emotions get even harder to swallow. It feels good to breath, relax, get enough rest, take a bath, or go outside. As soon as the excuses start in your mind, know that is your ego trying to keep you from losing its grip on you. The lower it can get your emotions, the easier it is to create dramatic stories in your mind that will ultimately come true because your ego has you obsessing over them.

Now, how would you begin to find your still point? The spaces between the spaces?

In your own words write a commitment to yourself to seek your inner truth and practice self-love. Express as many emotions as possible of how it would feel to have this as your starting point each day.

17

Separating Mind and Heart

"Life is dualistic, therefore use your heart as your guiding compass." ~ Sarah Breen

"Leading with the light of passion, we can never lose our way." ~ Leslie Baker

We stand at a crucial juncture now, a moment before the bend in the road reveals a new vision. We have guided you in the art of thinking—using your intellect to distinguish the ego's noise from the heart's gentle prompts. It requires a steadfast commitment: to love yourself without condition, to accept others wherever they are on their path, and to simply be the pure light you truly are—energy manifested in a tangible realm. Your external circumstances should not dictate your internal state, yet the world outside mirrors the collective inner landscapes of all.

In Western thought, the belief prevails that answers lie in perpetual thinking and activity. This notion perhaps traces back to Descartes, who famously declared, "I think, therefore I am." Yet, he only skimmed the surface of the mind's potential. The Buddha, by contrast, delved beyond mere thought into the realm of profound stillness, awaiting directions from the soul. He recognized the necessity of harmonizing mind and spirit, transcending dualistic existence.

It's not about segregating mind from heart but mastering conscious coexistence with both. Identifying whether you are mind-led—sleep-walking through life—or heart-led—awakening to true existence. This journey favors feeling over speaking; language often becomes a barrier as individual egos interpret words through diverse lenses. The perceived prison of your reality is constructed from your mind, ego, and entrenched beliefs. As you progress, you will glimpse the life's illusion, Maya—the deceptive self. Daily, we don costumes, our bodies, mistaking them for our essence. By distancing yourself from this facade, you recognize that external forces should not disrupt your inner peace. The deeper you probe the silent currents moving within, the more the veil of illusion dissipates. To truly embrace life and spirit, acknowledge this existence as a precious gift, knowing that true answers resonate in the quietude of your consciousness.

Life's essence isn't reaching a pinnacle but savoring the voyage—the true longing of the heart. Embrace a dynamic faith, one that finds assurance in the heart's leaps into the unknown, for these leaps afford you the essence of BEING. Experience each step, swaying with life's inherent dualities, and shed the resistance to the uncertain. Resistance nourishes the ego with incessant thoughts, fabricating fears of what might be. Instead, let your heart guide you into acceptance, welcoming life's dual nature. How can one recognize awakening without ever having slept? At times, we need to drift from awareness to appreciate the contrast. Honor the necessity of balancing mind and spirit. As

Asian monastic wisdom suggests, "the mind is a splendid servant but a dreadful master." This highlights the intrinsic desire to lead with what resonates at your core. Thought serves well when it syncs with the heart, but if tethered solely to sensory experiences, it amplifies the ego's fears. View this journey as a blossoming lotus, its heart the gem of existence. Know yourself more profoundly in silence than words could ever convey. That silence is your true center.

Choosing Heart or Mind

Life's duality can be likened to a pendulum's swing. The more energy you invest in its motion, the more extreme its arcs, yet it never halts at the midpoint. Thus, we must learn to temper the pendulum's momentum to find balance at the center. Life is a lesson in recognizing when you are awake—recalling your true essence—and when you are asleep—operating from mere intellect. If you venture too far in either direction of this duality, you risk being engulfed by shadows. It is within these shadows that growth potential lies, urging us not to ignore but to explore them.

Before addressing the questions that follow, take a moment to find your center. Set a timer and sit in quietude until the mental noise subsides. Should you fall asleep, that is what was needed. If the chatter persists, that too is where you are. Start there, delve into the emotions that surface, and endeavor to reach the deepest recesses of your mind.

What is the overarching theme you feel when exploring your still point? Write down as many feelings that you feel during this activity.

From your list of emotions, what do you feel is true (heart centered) and what do you feel is from the ego (mind)?

____

____

How often do these types of emotions take control and do they take shape in reoccurring situations? Explain.

____

____

____

____

____

____

____

____

____

____

____

____

____

Now for one of the deepest questions you could ask yourself at this point: Who is the person that wears the mask of me? Who is the stillness that walks this illusion everyday? What emotions describe your core within the stillness? Take your time

____

____

____

____

____

18

The Truth of it All

"Seeking is not guiding, but guidance from the heart can be found when you seek it." ~ Sarah Breen

"We always had the wings to fly." ~ Leslie Baker

Our society relentlessly pursues truth. As the horizon unfurls before you, the spirit's fruits become palpable. You are called to ascend into an exalted state of love and joy. Experience the richness of your spirit and navigate the external world with an internal spiral of love and joy. You may encounter those who shy away from your presence, as their egos perceive the luminescence of your inner world. Conversely, others will be drawn to you as they commence their awakening from the deep slumber of illusion. Embrace the duality of your existence, where your manifestations spring forth from your internal realm. If the external world displeases you, turn your focus inward. Shun actions that detach you from your spirit. In today's world, battles rage against various foes: hunger, disease, terrorism, and more. These conflicts mirror the turmoil within each individual's soul. Eventually, everyone arrives at a pivotal crossroad: follow the masses or emerge from the shadows to embrace the light? The light may initially blind you, but allow yourself time to adapt, and clarity will emerge.

Albert Einstein was a profound figure who delved beyond the cognitive realm to tap into the transcendental force pulsing through all consciousness—liberation from the mind and ego. He intellectualized transcendental meditation, discovering tranquility within our core. He identified this state as "pure being," an effortless and natural existence. Although it may take years, the intentions set with your heart lead to experiences that nourish your spirit over your ego. To awaken, you must first recognize your slumber; we repeatedly fall asleep at life's wheel, only to relish the joy of rediscovery—the pure bliss of existence without attachment or desire.

What are we illustrating here? Consider John Godfrey Saxe's poem, "The Blind Men and the Elephant," which analogizes our discussion. Six blind men, each touching a different part of an elephant, claim to understand the entire beast based on their limited experience. One feels the elephant's side and declares it a wall; another, feeling the tusk, says it's a spear; a third, touching the trunk, believes it's a snake; and so on. This story reflects our exploration of truth—whether in mythology, theology, philosophy, or spirituality, each perspective offers only a fragment of the whole. True understanding comes from within, from engaging in the work to uncover deeper truths.

Our collective yearning for enlightenment often stems from the ego rather than the heart. The quest for spiritual advancement, too, can be an ego-driven endeavor. Yet, as Einstein observed, the true process is effortless and natural. While many names and techniques describe this journey, it involves a harmonious effort of both mind and spirit to transcend into states of pure being, love, and joy. Your unique path will unfold through focus and a willingness to let go, allowing the mind to bridge to the spirit. You are never alone on this journey. Engage with your thoughts, then release them, letting your consciousness soar to the realms of pure being. Amidst the busyness imposed by your mind, it is crucial to connect with your center and awaken to your truth—a truth that is uniquely yours and felt deeply within. As you attune to your inner world, your external reality will mirror this inner alignment.

Imagine a life evolved into pure love. Envision the transformation that could unfold if you distanced yourself from the collective and embraced the radiance of the unknown.

Keep your ego in check and cherish the intricate dance of duality and unfolding. Pursue your curiosity, follow your heart, and listen more to the gentle inner nudges that have always been present. Remember, you are not broken and don't need fixing. It is simply time to realize that you have never been disconnected—only asleep at the wheel, with your heart patiently waiting for your awakening. Embrace the clarity, then continue to rediscover and renew. Your personal journey of mind and spirit is uniquely your own. **Recognize that while the mind is an excellent tool, your spirit—your heart, your center—is the true guide.**

Feel it!

As you commit to this path, you'll soon realize that you cannot escape your intentions, whether consciously or subconsciously set. If your current reality displeases you, understand that it is merely the manifestation of past thoughts and intentions. To alter your world, you must begin by addressing what pulses from within. From this point on, you can no longer hide from yourself; you know too much to remain inactive.

What does a heightened state of love and joy look and feel like to you?

____

____

____

____

____

____

____

____

____

____

____

____

____

If your outer world is a reflect of your inner world, what do you immediately commit to changing from this point forward? Explain

____

____

____

____

____

____

____

____

____

____

____

____

____

____

Take something that comes natural to you, something that you disregard as a talent, you just love to do it. Understand that this is what it is like to feel pure being. It's a flow that is effortless and natural to you. Describe what comes natural to you and what you feel during that process?

____

____

____

____

____

____

____

____

____

____

____

____

____

____

———————————————————————————
———————————————————————————
———————————————————————————
———————————————————————————
———————————————————————————
———————————————————————————
———————————————————————————
———————————————————————————
———————————————————————————
———————————————————————————

Bookmark that feeling in your mind and heart. This is the tip of the iceberg when it comes to meditation. What is natural and effortless to you is an open channel for you spirit to work through. Your ego wants to disregard it, pay no attention to those voices. Sit that ego in the corner and turn it around so you don't pay any attention to it. Go back a reread what you wrote to feel it in your heart.

After reading the "Blind Men and the Elephant", how has your perception of you beliefs and yourself changed?

———————————————————————————
———————————————————————————
———————————————————————————
———————————————————————————
———————————————————————————
———————————————————————————
———————————————————————————
———————————————————————————
———————————————————————————

What is your perception of the process to pure being?

19

Putting it Together

"Earth School is the opportunity to ripple your greatest gifts. Use your mind as a tool and let it be guided by your heart." ~ Sarah Breen

"Every soul who walks the path on this Earth holds the key to a light so unique and special it begs to be seen. Feel this truth light up the veins that run through your body, and allow your gifts to be shared with the world." ~ Leslie Baker

This process gives you a starting point, the map to your unfoldment will be unique to you. Are you ready to see what it looks like? We've given you the steps to guide you along your journey, to help you refocus when needed, and give you the empowerment to listen to your heart. Your map will allow you to recalibrate the ego so you can easily listen and feel your true nature, which means that the steps you take will be yours, and yours alone.

Here's how to start:

1: Why am I here? Because deep down, you sense life is more than what you see. You're not disconnected; you are asleep at the wheel. In fact, you conformed to a reality sculpted by your ego, your conditioning. The only control you have is to relinquish the filters in your mind, recalibrating the ego that holds tight to this physical reality. This is the first step of realizing you may not know who you really are. This may be scary. You must admit now you have been asleep.

2: Ask yourself the right questions:

What does this mean to me?
What was the prominent feeling in this situation?
What would I want to feel instead?

These questions help you understand where you are and where your conditioned mind is taking you. From here you begin to compartmentalize what is truly from the heart and what stems from conditioned circumstance. If you tend to seek out pleasure to avoid pain, focus on what others think of you, or seek out distractions or other stimuli because you cannot be fulfilled without it... then you have to recognize you're asleep. Realizing these behaviors feed your ego to only keep you asleep is part of this process. Don't label them, just let them be, allow them to fall away and be ok with filling the spaces with silence holding a space for your true self to come through. Don't put your head in the sand when you see your patterns and not be willing to change them.

You must be willing to let go of the old patterns, the structure that has been built to keep you DOING and not BEING. You are limitless! Some part of you knows this is true.

3: Purpose: Reflect on your life's endeavors not to question your past but to review it. Identify the moments when your actions weren't ego-driven but were intuitively guided, like when you lost track of time or stood up for yourself unknowingly. This discovery is crucial for shedding others' expectations and embracing your true desires.

4: Vision: Feel from your heart and KNOW what your core values are. What does your gut tell you is important to you? Those are the soft nudges through the cracks of the ego to help you find your way back to your heart. Use your mind and put aside all that you know and open the flood gates to imagine the "what if..." life without limitations. Exercise your mind into a new perspective, one that is full of the well-being and peace you desire. This is where things like vision boards, automatic-writing, and scrap booking can be helpful.

5: Decision: This is you learning to say NO to what no longer serves you and YES to your inner self, your spirit, your heart. This isn't about drastic life changes but about granting yourself the liberty to venture into the unknown. You must question everything you become aware of. Your questioning alone will create the change you're looking for. Go beyond your questioning and go into your feelings. Feel for the sticky points and then feel for the love, it will never steer you wrong. Keep your mind away from what you think is your current reality and feel from your heart as you make decisions. Things should inspire and excite you with a healthy amount of fear. Go with your gut and don't allow the fear to block you.

6: **Handling the Blocks:** If you feel something is blocking you, you're right. If you feel there is a gate that you must open; you're right. The blocks, gates, or any images that you feel are in your way exist in your mind. The conditioned mind holds tightly to paradigms that have constructed the illusion of self. The ego is the identification of the self so you must realize that the conditioned behaviors are not yours to begin with: they are something you have adopted through the guidance of society. It is now your job to drop them, question them, doubt them, and let them go one by one. Each time you drop one, you will be able to look at life and make decisions from the perspective of your heart, your true self, and less from your mind and ego.

7: **Use the Mind as a TOOL:** Thinking is a wonderful tool when it is used as a servant to the heart. Question EVERYTHING your mind brings into focus while using the spiritual assets. You were born with no preconceived perception of reality, then grew up learning everyone else's perceptions and have spent the rest of your life trying to dismantle those very perceptions that have shaped your ego to date. Some people fear that they will lose their identity in this process. Instead, know that you will gain a sense of autonomy that cannot be tampered with by anyone else. The ego thrives on creating barriers, everything is either good or bad to it. Your heart is unique and will vibrate out such a uniqueness that the acknowledgment of others will no longer matter as you are completely fulfilled in any situation.

8: **The Fear, Faith, & Beliefs:** This is the test before the gates of the awakened consciousness, the heart. This is the moment when you decide to jump into the unknown but KNOW that you will float on the other side. Walking in the dark and knowing your footing is strong and safe. This is following your heart and holding your focus on the heart. If you are afraid, your mind is controlling the situation. If you have doubts, your beliefs are doubting the decision. If you have faith, you are stepping off the ledge KNOWING there is a place to land on. That is where freedom really is. It has never been about self-development or self-improvement, it has only been about dismantling the self, the ego, and recognizing the heart center.

9: **The focus point is in the silence:** The source of all being is a still point or your own personal, magical black hole, your access point to Source. It's where everything is still but yet it is still moving. It is where you focus on yourself or an object until it completely disappears in your mind. You may come face-to-face with the pain, but that's okay: the pain is the feelings you work through as you allow the candle to burn on both ends. To follow your heart, you must create focus points that are in alignment with where you are and where you want to be. The feelings are what we must focus in tandem with the inner dialog you have with yourself. This will help you identify and compartmentalize the ego and allow it to drop away.

10: **Allowing:** This is the practice of letting go of resistance. Our mind is what creates the resistance. Any feelings that do not feel good are created from the mind, the self. Notice how many headaches or stomach pains you get when you are stressed out or worried. Sometimes, your heart literally hurts. You have created so much resistance that it is affecting you on a physical level. The art of detachment and knowing what you are responsible for will help you in holding a space for your true nature to shine through. You will find your heart in the still point, the inward movement of the silence that will give you the peace you need right now to move forward. This process takes time and willingness on your part shed the old and explore what lies beyond what your mind has identified as you. The worse you feel, the more resistance; the better you feel, the less resistance.

11: **Finding what works for you**: Every thought has created our world and has created your experiences. The ego sees everything as good or bad. The ego requires a barrier at all times. This entire process is about dismantling the ego slowly, so it does not fight you at the gates of the awakened consciousness: your truth. This process of dismantling the ego has been done through techniques like transcendental meditation, chanting, ceremonies, hallucinogenic medicines, etc. The use of techniques is helpful in the dismantling process but be warned that when the techniques themselves become a desire or need to perform them then the ego has its grip on them and is trying to take you away from the gate of your truth. You WILL fall asleep at the wheel... that's part of the process. You WILL never be fully awakened all the time... that is part of this human experience. But you CAN and WILL make MASSIVE change within yourself, your environment, and ultimately your life for the positive.

12: **When in doubt, follow the heart:** At times during this process, you may feel that you don't know who you are. That's because you have identified yourself with what your ego has created your entire life. This can create an inner imbalance that fosters many of the unwanted experiences in your life. Don't be afraid of what you don't know about yourself. Coming from a neutral state, a loving state, a state of an empty glass humbly waiting for the stillness to dance with you around grandfather fire, get ready to jump across the fire and transcend into the eternalness that has been available to you since the beginning of time. It's a breath away, a practiced space of holding, a channel that will make you feel nothing but everything at the same time. You will be freed of perspectives and be opened to freely find new perspectives that do not create more control from the ego. Everything transcends through you and out of you like a clear vessel. Thought is not a bad thing; it is a TOOL to use in this lifetime to distinguish the heart or soul's direction.

Key Points to Remember:

1. You don't know what you don't know.
2. Look at yourself with a new lens of perception: "I am LOVE, I am eternal, I am transcending."
3. Realize that you are wearing a mask of illusion, but we chose to wear it and play the part: it's the human experience.
4. Pure love and joy are expansive... you can and will expand with it as it's the way of the heart.
5. You can create more change in yourself and your surroundings when you act from an inner peace instead of reacting to circumstances.

Black Elk of the Lakota tribe stated in the book of *The First Peace; My Search for the better Angels* by Charles Wilson Hatfield: "The first peace, which is the most important, is that which comes from within the souls of ... (people) when they realize their relationship, their oneness with the universe and all its Powers, and when they realize that at the center of the universe, dwells ... (the Great Mystery), and that this center is really everywhere, it is within each of us. This is the real Peace, and the others are but reflections of this. The second peace is that which is made between two individuals, and the third is that which is made between two nations. But above all, you should understand that there can never be peace between nations until there is first known that true peace which is within ... (our) souls ..."

Black Elk said it profoundly, that what you are reaching for is within you. That you must go inward and find the inner stillness to make the shift to peace. It starts with the first peace, you.

Where Do We Go From Here?

Let's summarize and ask some key questions to bring it all together. Notice that some of your answers may have already changed from the time you started this process to now the new beginning. Take a moment to answer the questions below and then go back to reread your thoughts from the beginning of the workbook till now. It will demonstrate to you how quickly you can find your truth by just tapping on the spigot in our hearts. I encourage you to reach out with your experiences, share with our community, and pass it on to others. The world needs more enlightened souls on its side.

Why am I here?

____

____

____

____

____

____

____

____

____

____

____

What are the right questions you need to ask yourself? When do you need to be asking yourself them?

____

____

____

____

____

____

____

____

____

____

____

What have you uncovered so far to be your purpose?

____

____

____

____

____

____

____

____

Use your vision in your imagination to feel from your heart to what it is you desire the most to experience?

What do you need to practice saying NO to? What are the things you need to start saying YES to more often? (hint: self-care)

What are you going to do about those blocks now? What are they really?

How are you going to utilize your mind as a TOOL?

How can you turn your fears and beliefs into complete faith?

What have you decided to be your focus points and how do you find them?

What is the process of allowing yourself to feel from your heart?

What activities work for you, right now, in finding your heart center? Try not to take on and learn something completely new. Start today by using something that is natural and effortless and add a new piece to it that will help you evolve up the spiral. Taking something completely new will put too much mind into it and the heart will be softer.

After reading Black Elk's quote, what do you feel is the most important aspect you are called to work with first? Explain your answer

This COMPLETE GUIDE has been an attempt to explain what is limitless, what is beyond your conditioned mind, what is in your spirit. It is timeless, boundless, all-knowing without need. Words cannot teach nor can it begin to explain an experience that can only be felt within your center, one that is profoundly unique to your nature. Seeking the right definition only allows your ego to grab toward something else it wants to control. Allow the process to unfold without effort. This is an effortless state of being found within the heart of each person. A tug and pull process of mind and heart. A focus within the mind and an allowing of the heart to take the center. It's not what you think, and it will blow your thinking away each time because the mind cannot construct what is limitless.

It has been an attempt to help you dissect your mind, awaken from your slumber, and delve into your unique emotions and situations. Your core truth loves you more than words can express. This thought, when connected to your heart, will make you cry tears of joy. When the mind and heart meet, it creates an electrical current so intense that only that feeling can be felt; thoughts do not exist in the same moment. Your spirit, your heart center, is your truth. This natural and effortless process will take time, but the universe sees you as it always has. You're just now aware that you are seen. Open your heart, use your mind as a tool, feel from your heart, and make peace with yourself. Only then can we make our future as vibrant as it is meant to be.

Life is a beautiful gift, one in which we were granted the ability to forget what we once knew, and then experience the remembering. It's a beautiful unfolding of realization, awakening, remembering, and being who you really are NOW. Awaken from your slumber and unfold. Your map is unique. All you have to do is decide, listen, and embark on this journey of remembering. The world needs you to step forward and reignite your truth.

Live Your Medicine,

Sarah Breen

Sarah Breen, known as The Earth School Shaman, is deeply committed to the path of Earth Medicine, facilitating profound reconnections to our deepest memories and the essence of our being. Through her transformative journey from the brink of suicide to a vibrant life enriched with spiritual connections, Sarah has uncovered her core purpose—to unleash the inherent potential within each of us by deconditioning the mental and emotional bindings that tether our hearts.

An Advanced Master in Shamanic Energy Medicine Practitioner, Sarah's expertise also includes being an International Best Selling Author, Certified Shamanic Lightworker, Yuen Practitioner, Munay-Ki Practitioner, and Reiki Master. She has extensive training in interfaith religion studies among various healing modalities. Additionally, Sarah practices as a Licensed Massage Therapist, animal intuitive, and certified animal massage therapist, always exploring how energy influences our physical, mental, and spiritual health.

With over 18 years of experience navigating the energy realms of Spirit, Sarah's teachings reconnect us to our roots in Earth Medicine. She advocates for a shift from merely describing spiritual experiences to actively participating in them, urging us to live through our hearts and engage with life's mysteries directly.

Dedicated to healing not just individuals but the collective, Sarah understands the impact of personal transformation on communal consciousness. Her daily rituals honor her ancestors and the broader ancestral community, helping to awaken and release the suppressed fears, beliefs, and traumas within us.

As a mother of two young boys, Sarah is passionate about altering how unresolved energies from our past influence our children's futures. Her holistic practices promote conscious living that clears pathways and builds bridges for future generations to advance unencumbered by humanity's old wounds. She envisions a world where our children can leap forward, free from the chains that once bound us.

Sarah believes that healing is a choice—one that lets us access the necessary healing exactly where we are. Her role as a Munay-Ki Practitioner is to activate your potential and provide tools that foster a journey of heart-aligned action, unconditional love, and clear, insightful thinking. Guiding you along your authentic path, Sarah reminds us that true healing demands walking in integrity and authenticity. Her mission in "Unhinge Yourself" is not just to heal but to liberate—to unhinge the mind from old beliefs and free the heart from past pains, enabling each of us to live fully and freely as our true selves.

www.EarthSchoolShaman.com

About the Illustrator

Cover Illustrator Leslie Baker worked several years creating intuitive art for clients. Drawing portraits based on the visions and energy she would receive. Leslie also has a long career as a Fashion Designer, and continues to do this work, along with painting, embroidery and her digital art. She currently lives in Wisconsin. She can be reached at Leslie.Baker76@gmail.com

Unhinge Yourself: Embracing Your Authentic Medicine Through the Shamanic Wheel

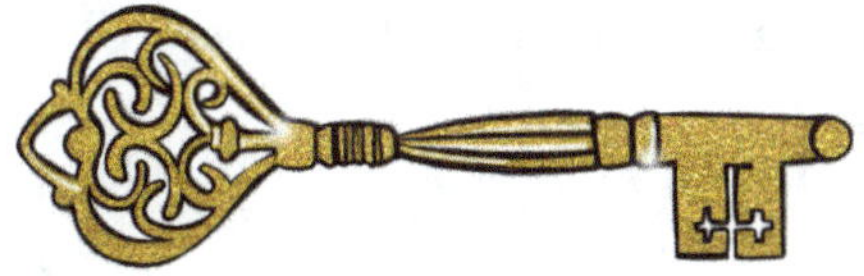

In the relentless hustle of modern life, the vision for your true self can become obscured. Like a wheel stuck in the mud, the mind spins, and the heart yearns for something more profound.

Have you ever awoken in the night, pondering a way out, questioning where you've gone astray? You've followed the prescribed path of X, Y, and Z, only to find it leads nowhere fulfilling. Our society dictates success through compliance and acquisition, yet seldom do these align with our authentic selves.

Unhinge Yourself - Live Your Medicine Authentically invites you on a shamanic journey through the medicine wheel, a sacred map guiding you back to your core essence, the authentic voice buried beneath layers of conditioning. This voice whispers of your unique medicine, your true calling, waiting to be reclaimed.

Carl Jung once said, "Your vision becomes clear only when you can look into your own heart. Who looks outside, dreams; who looks inside, awakes." This journey invites you to awaken, to explore the depths of your being and reclaim the power that is inherently yours.

Do societal expectations cage you? Do you grapple with boundaries, communication, and overwhelming emotions? If you're ready to shed the weights of guilt, shame, and exhaustion to embrace authenticity, this is where your transformation begins.

Through the **Unhinge Yourself** program, you will:

- **Cease People-Pleasing:** Forge healthy boundaries, empowering yourself to put your needs first without the shadow of guilt.
- **Navigate Life's Triggers:** Develop strategies to maintain calm and clarity, even in the stormiest interactions.
- **Release Blocks:** Clear out misaligned beliefs that cloud your relationships and self-understanding, paving the way for clarity and freedom.
- **Embrace Authenticity:** Cultivate the courage to be unapologetically you, enjoying the liberation from fear of judgment and the burdens of emotional toil.
- **Transform Relationships:** Heal old wounds and forge meaningful connections that honor your true self.
- **Discover Your Purpose:** Unearth and step confidently into your unique calling, free from the chains of self-doubt.

This program includes:

- **Personalized One-on-One Sessions:** Deep dive into healing with Sarah through sacred, transformative sessions that address the roots of your wounds, help reclaim your power, and align you with your authenticity.
- **Rich Course Materials:** Engage with audio sessions, meditative practices, and profound shamanic exercises designed to deepen your connection to self and spirit.
- **A Journey Through the Medicine Wheel:** Traverse the directions of the Shamanic Map of Authenticity—each bearing potent teachings from the Serpent, Wolf, Bear, Raven, and the Crystal Skull to assist in discovering and living your medicine.

Are you prepared to transform your life? To stop spinning and start being? To reclaim the essence of your human spirit? If these words stir something within you, it's time to step forward. Scan the QR code to embark on the **Unhinge Yourself** program, and reclaim the medicine of your soul.